Catherine Atkinson has a degree in Food and Nutrition BSc (Hons). She has been Deputy Cookery Editor on *Woman's Weekly* magazine and later Cookery Editor of *Home*. Catherine is now a full-time writer and food consultant to various lifestyle and health magazines and has written more than sixty cookbooks.

CALGARY PUBLIC LIBRARY

OCT 2019

OTHER TITLES

Fermenting Food for Healthy Eating
Power Blending and Juicing
How To Make Your Own Cordials and Syrups
How To Make Perfect Panini
Everyday Bread from Your Bread Machine
The High Speed Blender Cookbook
Everyday Family Recipes for Your Combination Microwave

Cooking With Your Instant Pot

Catherine Atkinson

A HOW TO BOOK

ROBINSON

ROBINSON

First published in Great Britain in 2018 by Robinson

Copyright © Catherine Atkinson, 2018

10 9 8 7 6 5 4 3 2 1

The moral right of the author has been asserted.

All rights reserved.
No part of this publication may be reproduced, stored in a retrieval system, or transmitted, in any form, or by any means, without the prior permission in writing of the publisher, nor be otherwise circulated in any form of binding or cover other than that in which it is published and without a similar condition including this condition being imposed on the subsequent purchaser.

A CIP catalogue record for this book is available from the British Library.

ISBN: 978-1-47214-261-0

Typeset by Basement Press, Glaisdale
Printed and bound in Great Britain by CPI Group (UK) Ltd, Croydon CR0 4YY

Papers used by Robinson are from well-managed forests and other responsible sources.

MIX
Paper from responsible sources
FSC
www.fsc.org
FSC® C104740

Robinson
An imprint of
Little, Brown Book Group
Carmelite House
50 Victoria Embankment
London EC4Y 0DZ

An Hachette UK Company
www.hachette.co.uk

www.littlebrown.co.uk

How To Books are published by Robinson, an imprint of Little, Brown Book Group. We welcome proposals from authors who have first-hand experience of their subjects. Please set out the aims of your book, its target market and its suggested contents in an email to howtobooks@littlebrown.co.uk

Contents

INTRODUCTION

Your Instant Pot is a multi-functional modern electric pressure cooker. It also works as a slow cooker, rice cooker, yogurt maker and steamer. Safe and dependable, it uses up to 70 per cent less energy than a conventional oven, and makes cooking faster and more convenient.

Pressure cookers have evolved so much over the last few decades. Once these large and slightly feared hissing machines sat on top of the hob and needed frequent attention. Your modern-day stainless-steel Instant Pot, with its removable and dish-washable inner pot, is sleek and compact and can be simply plugged into a convenient socket on your worktop, ready to cook at the push of a button. Unlike a slow cooker, you can also sauté, brown and reheat food by using the Sauté button on a low, medium or high setting. After cooking, a 'Keep Warm' function means that your meal will stay hot until you are ready to eat.

This book will show you how to make the most of your Instant Pot and cook with confidence. You'll discover how to create a range of healthy, easy-to-make meals, from delicious breakfasts and brunches, soups and no-fuss suppers, midweek and special-occasion mains to decadent-tasting desserts. Altogether, there are more than 125 recipes to make with minimum effort and maximum taste.

Perfect for both beginners and those who are already enthusiasts of this fantastic machine, you'll find all the information and guidance you need to make the most of your Instant Pot.

GETTING STARTED

After unpacking your Instant Pot, you'll be keen to get cooking, but all the different buttons (more about those later) can seem a little daunting at first. Before you start, give your new machine a test run. This will not only familiarise you with the way it works, but will also make sure that everything is running smoothly as it should.

Have a good look at the illustration of all your Instant Pot's parts in the manufacturer's booklet and check that the Pressure (steam) Release switch (this is the black knob that sticks up, with a little penguin-like wing) and Float Valve (the silicone-covered knob on the inside of the lid which can be gently pulled up and down) are unobstructed and clean and that the clear silicone sealing ring is properly inserted. This is on the underside of the lid and fits on the inner rim; when correctly inserted you will be able to gently slide it round without it sticking. You should quickly check these every time you use your machine.

1   Place the stainless-steel inner pot in the cooker base (it's probably packed in there already, so lift it out and make sure all plastic wrapping and padding is removed) and pour in about 1 litre (1¾ pints) water. Generally, either hot or cold water can be used. It takes a little longer to come to pressure if cold water is used, so in some cases it's better to use boiling water (cakes, for example, which need to start cooking immediately), and where preferred this is mentioned in the recipe.

2   Put on the lid, turning until it fits into the closed position (the steam release and float valve go on the opposite side to the control panel; the lid won't fit the other way round). The arrows at the front will show you which way to turn the lid to lock it into place. Turn the pressure-release switch to the 'Sealing' mark on the lid (there are two options: 'Sealing' and 'Venting').

3   Press the 'Steam' button, then press the minus button to set the cooking time to 1 minute (if you press and hold down the buttons, they change more quickly). Your Instant Pot is then programmed and you don't need to do anything else until the cooking cycle is complete.

4   After 10 seconds, your Instant Pot will start the preheating cycle and the display will show 'On'. Within a few minutes, steam will release for a minute or two until the Float Valve

pops up to seal the cooker. Once pressure is reached (which will take around 10 minutes), the countdown timer will begin.

5 When the cycle is complete, the machine will bleep and automatically switch to the 'Keep Warm' mode. Press the 'Keep Warm/Cancel' button. Once the pot cools down (which will take around 10 minutes), you can open the lid, tip out the water and start cooking.

WHAT ALL THE BUTTONS MEAN

Your Instant Pot will have many buttons and will probably include Soup, Meat/Stew, Bean/Chili, Poultry and Porridge. The most important thing to realise is that while these programmes may differ very slightly in the way that they heat, they all have pre-set suggested times for that particular food.

If, for example, you press the Poultry button, your Instant Pot cannot tell how much is in the pot, or whether the food is at room temperature or frozen, chopped into small pieces or one large chicken, so will not be able to sense when food is cooked through. You will therefore need to adjust the time to suit the dish you are cooking, as default times will rarely match the cooking time you require. You may find it easier, especially when you start to use your Instant Pot, to use the Manual or Pressure Cook button most of the time (your machine will have one or other of these buttons but not both).

The **Manual** or **Pressure Cook** function can be adjusted to any time and switched between High and Low pressure. If you want Manual (Pressure Cook) with High Pressure, press Manual (Pressure Cook), then if the pressure isn't already on High (this will depend on the last time you cooked in your Instant Pot), press Pressure until it changes to High Pressure mode. Finally, adjust the time by pressing the '+' or '−' (again, the time that comes up will depend on the last time you cooked).

The **Steam** function heats continuously and gets hotter faster than any other setting which has cycles that turn on and off. This fast heating is particularly useful for quick-cooking foods such as vegetables and seafood.

The **Rice** function is the only fully-automated programme. It always cooks on low pressure and the time is predetermined by the amount of rice that is in the pot and cannot be changed. This setting is only suitable for long-grain white and easy-cook white rice.

The **Multigrain** function takes much longer to pressurise than other settings; this allows grains to soak and start absorbing liquid before cooking commences.

The **Yogurt** function has two components: one for heating (sterilising) the milk and a second part that incubates it.

The **Slow Cook** function works like a typical slow cooker. It has three temperature settings which you access by pressing Slow Cook, then 'Adjust': Less for the lowest temperature, between 82°C and 89°C (180°F–190°F), Normal for a medium temperature, between 88°C and 93°C (190°F–200°F) and More for a high temperature, between 93°C and 99°C (200°F–210°F). The lowest setting will only keep food warm; it isn't suitable for cooking foods.

The **Sauté** function can be set by pressing 'Sauté', then 'Adjust' to change the temperature from Less, a low heat ideal for simmering liquids, Normal, a medium heat for sautéing, and More, a high heat for fast-frying and browning foods such as meat. The time will default to 30 minutes and is not changeable, so when if you only want to sauté for a few minutes, you will need to press the Keep Warm/Cancel button to turn off the Sauté function.

Do not use your Instant Pot lid with the Sauté function; you can use a glass pan lid with steam hole (see page 5) if you want.

PRESSURE-COOKING BASICS

In conventional cooking, whether on the hob or in the oven, general water-based cooking will only reach a temperature of 100°C (212°F). At that point, water boils and turns to steam and some will evaporate even if the pot is covered with a lid. Inside a sealed pressure cooker, the steam can't escape and this increases the pressure inside the pot and the temperature rises.

In your Instant Pot, low pressure is between 6 and 7psi (pounds per square inch) with a temperature between 110°C and 112°C (230°F and 233°F). High pressure is between 10.2 and 11.6psi and the temperature between 115°C and 118°C (240°F and 245°F). When the pot comes to pressure, the liquid inside isn't boiling but is hotter. This is vital when cooking foods such as meat, as long boiling would make it tough. It is only when the pressure is released – either naturally, or quickly by opening the steam vent (see page 00) – that the liquid will begin to boil. For this reason, you should always open the lid with care.

Liquid is essential when you are pressure-cooking, but remember that since there is virtually no evaporation you will need a little less than when cooking conventionally.

GETTING EQUIPPED

Your Instant Pot will come with an easy-to-clean and dish-washable stainless-steel inner pot, a stainless-steel trivet (steaming rack) and a fitted silicone sealing ring. These are the only pieces of equipment you will need for basic cooking, but there are other useful items you may already have or wish to buy.

Extra sealing rings. Silicone sealing rings are prone to picking up odours such as spices and curry and this may be a minor problem when you come to making foods such as yogurt and desserts. Very occasionally, and usually after very long use, your sealing ring may get damaged or stretched and need replacing (you cannot use your Instant Pot without the sealing ring). It is therefore worth considering buying an extra sealing ring or two. As well as plain colourless sealing rings, you can also buy packs of two different colours so that you can use specific rings for savoury and sweet recipes.

Glass lid with steam hole. This is particularly useful when you are making yogurt or simmering or reheating soups, sauces or casseroles or when you want to cover your Instant Pot during sautéing. Check your pan lids before purchasing as you may already have a size that fits.

Non-stick inner pot. This is handy if you want to sauté in a minimum amount of fat or oil and when making porridge, rice pudding and similar milky foods, as milk proteins tend to stick when they cook.

Silicone tins with tempered glass bases. You can use ordinary metal tins in your Instant Pot (always make sure they fit first), but frequent use may affect non-stick linings and coatings on some tins. You can purchase silicone 'tins' with tempered glass bases (never use ordinary glass in your Instant Pot when using as a pressure cooker; heatproof glass is fine when using as a slow cooker), which are ideal for making cheesecakes, desserts and foods such as meatloaf. Make sure that they are intended for use with your Instant Pot.

Metal bowl. Useful for making foods by steam such as dulce de leche, which would burn if cooked directly in the inner pot.

Steamer basket. Although your Instant Pot will come with a trivet (steaming rack), a stainless-steel steamer basket is useful for steaming vegetables and small items such as dim sum. You can also buy steamers that have dividers to steam several types of vegetable separately at the same time.

Egg-steaming racks. If you only want to cook a few 'boiled' eggs occasionally (see page 18), simply cook them on your trivet (steaming rack). If you cook 'boiled' eggs regularly, you may want to invest in an egg-steaming rack with a hole for each egg. You can also buy stackable racks which allow you to cook up to fourteen eggs at a time.

Foil sling. Essential for lifting out tins safely and easily, you can't buy these, but they are simple to make. Take a piece of foil about 55cm (22in) long and 15cm (6in) wide – it doesn't have to be exact. Fold it in half lengthways, then fold again to make a sling. This will blacken slightly after use, but don't discard; let it dry and it can be used many times.

COOKING RICE AND GRAINS

One of the dedicated functions of your Instant Pot is as a rice cooker. It is intended for long-grain white rice and is fully automated: you simply add the rice (well-rinsed in a sieve under cold running water) and liquid plus any seasonings and flavourings, then press the Rice button; your Instant Pot will do the rest. For best results, measure out 1 part rice to 1¼ parts water or stock.

The following volume method is the easiest way to cook all other types of rice and grains in your Instant Pot.

Measure the required dry amount in a jug (allowing about 75g/3oz per person, a little more if you want larger portions). Make a note of the volume and use as a measure for the amount of liquid you will need to add. All rice and grains should be rinsed in cold water before adding to your Instant Pot, and a small amount of butter or oil added to the cooking liquid to prevent foaming. With the exception of white long-grain rice, grains and rice should be cooked with the Manual (Pressure Cook) function on High pressure.

	Liquid per measure of rice/grain	Minutes	Release
Arborio rice	1½	6	Quick release
Barley (pearl)	4	20	Natural release
Barley (pot)	3½	22	Natural release
Basmati white rice (soaked in cold water for 1 hour)	1	4	Natural for 5 minutes, then quick release
Brown rice	1½	12	Natural for 10 minutes, then quick release
Buckwheat	1¾	3	Natural release
Jasmine rice	1	5	Quick release
Quinoa	2	2	Quick release
Wild rice mix	2½	10	Natural release

COOKING DRIED BEANS AND PULSES

Your Instant Pot is brilliant for cooking dried beans and they can be cooked from dried. However, you'll get better results if you pre-soak the beans for at least 4 hours, or preferably overnight in plenty of cold water with salt – 5ml (1 tsp) salt per litre (1¾ pints) water. Soaking in lightly salted water will help ensure that the beans stay intact and there will be fewer broken skins.

Remember that dried beans double in volume and weight after soaking and cooking, so do not fill the inner pot more than half-full. If cooking beans from dried, use three times the volume of water to dried beans; when cooking pre-soaked beans, the water should come about 2.5cm (1in) above the beans. Either cook on the Bean/Chili setting or the Manual (Pressure Cook) setting. After cooking, allow the pressure to release naturally.

Beans	Dry Cooking time (minutes)	Pre-soaked Cooking time (minutes)
Aduki beans	20	12
Black beans	20	12
Black-eyed beans	22	14
Butter beans	20	12
Cannellini beans	35	20
Chickpeas	38	20
Green lentils	15	N/A
Kidney beans	25	20
Pinto or borlotti beans	25	20
Soya beans	30	21

FREQUENTLY ASKED QUESTIONS

How safe is my Instant Pot?

Extremely safe. Unlike old-fashioned pressure cookers, your Instant Pot has many built-in safety devices. It can detect if the lid isn't properly closed or if it is 'leaking' steam (either because the steam-release valve hasn't been closed properly or because the sealing ring is missing or isn't properly in place) and won't start pressurised cooking. Your cooker has a mechanism that can detect if you have not added enough liquid and will not reach pressure level; if preheating is unusually long, it will switch to the Keep Warm mode to prevent food burning. It also has a locked lid device to prevent you removing the lid until pressure has been completely released.

Why does cooking take longer than the time specified on the recipe?

The time that you enter on your Instant Pot control panel isn't the time it takes to cook a dish, as your Instant Pot needs to come to pressure before countdown starts. This depends on the quantity of liquid and the temperature of the contents; it will take longer if the ingredients are very cold or partially/completely frozen. After cooking is complete, you may need to allow extra time for natural pressure release.

What's the difference between 'natural pressure release' and 'quick pressure release' and when should they be used?

When pressure-cooking is complete, you can either leave your Instant Pot to depressurise naturally or turn the pressure-release valve/switch to 'Venting' to allow steam to escape and quickly release the pressure. Quick-release is great for quickly stopping the cooking process to prevent overcooking of foods such as vegetables and seafood.

Natural pressure release is better for keeping your kitchen steam-free and is ideal for foods such as soups, casseroles and meat dishes such as whole chicken, which benefit from 'resting' after cooking. You should always use natural pressure release for foods with a high starch content such as porridge, foods with a large liquid volume, or foamy food which might splutter through the vent if pressure is released quickly. Often recipes suggest a 5- or 10-minute natural pressure release, followed by a quick pressure release and this is a good compromise between the two.

How full can I fill my Instant Pot?

It depends on what you are cooking. When using your Instant Pot as a pressure cooker for making soups and casserole-type dishes, it should never be more than two-thirds full. With foods that foam, such as lentils, beans and pulses, or food that swells or expands, like grains and pasta, it should be no more than half-full. When using as a steamer to cook fish or cakes, it is fine to have the solid food higher in the pot, but it should still be below the 'max' line. When you are not cooking with pressure – slow-cooking for example – you can fill the inner pot up to the 'max' line.

If I want to double a recipe, should I also double the cooking time?

Most recipes in this book serve four people, but if you increase recipe quantities you do not need to increase cooking times – for example if you cook eight chicken drumsticks rather than four. You will find that your Instant Pot takes a little longer to come to pressure with a larger amount of food in the pot.

KEY TO SYMBOLS

 vegetarian

 vegan

CONVERSION CHARTS

WEIGHT

Metric	Imperial
25g	1oz
50g	2oz
75g	3oz
100g	4oz
150g	5oz
175g	6oz
200g	7oz
225g	8oz
250g	9oz
300g	10oz
350g	12oz
400g	14oz
450g	1lb

OVEN TEMPERATURES

Celsius	Fahrenheit
110°C	225°F
120°C	250°F
140°C	275°F
150°C	300°F
160°C	325°F
180°C	350°F
190°C	375°F
200°C	400°F
220°C	425°F
230°C	450°F
240°C	475°F

LIQUIDS

Metric	Imperial	Us Cup
5ml	1 tsp	1 tsp
15ml	1 tbsp	1 tbsp
50ml	2fl oz	3 tbsp
60ml	2½fl oz	¼ cup
75ml	3fl oz	⅓ cup
100ml	4fl oz	scant ½ cup
125ml	4½ oz	½ cup
150ml	5fl oz	⅔ cup
200ml	7fl oz	scant 1 cup
250ml	9fl oz	1 cup
300ml	½ pint	1¼ cups
350ml	12fl oz	1 ⅓ cups
400ml	¾ pint	1¾ cups
500ml	17fl oz	2 cups
600ml	1 pt	2½ cups

1

Breakfasts

Whether you are looking for a quick midweek breakfast or a more leisurely weekend brunch with family or friends, your Instant Pot will help you get ready to face the day. Here you'll find delicious cereals such as porridge, quinoa flakes and couscous, healthy home-made yogurt that can be enjoyed plain or quickly whizzed into smoothies, simple 'boiled' eggs and tasty omelettes. There's plenty of choice to give your energy levels a boost throughout the morning and keep you alert until lunchtime.

Proper Porridge

Forget stirring a pan of simmering oats on the hob, or making do with instant oats – your Instant Pot simplifies this popular breakfast cereal. While traditional porridge is made with just oats, water and a pinch of salt, the addition of milk – whichever type you like – adds a creamy consistency and extra nutrients to start the day.

SERVES 2 (OR MAKES A VERY GENEROUS PORTION FOR 1)

75g (3oz) jumbo 'old-fashioned' oats, or 65g (2½oz)
    rolled oats
450ml (¾ pint) milk, or almond or rice milk
    if you prefer, or a combination of milk and water
7g (¼oz) butter (optional)
Pinch of salt (optional)
2.5ml (½ tsp) ground cinnamon or 5ml (1 tsp) vanilla extract
    (optional), to flavour
Greek yogurt, fresh or dried fruit, chopped nuts, to serve
    (optional)
Honey, agave or maple syrup, or brown sugar, to drizzle
    (optional)

1   Put the oats in the inner pot and pour over the milk. Add the butter, cut into tiny pieces, if using, and a pinch of salt, if liked. Add additional flavourings such as ground cinnamon or vanilla extract, if liked. Stir briefly.
2   Put on the lid and lock into place. Turn the pressure-release switch to Sealing. Press the Porridge button, adjust the pressure to High and the time to 4 minutes if using jumbo oats, 3 minutes for rolled oats. After cooking, allow the pressure to release naturally (this will take 10–12 minutes).

3 Open the lid, stir the porridge and serve straight away. If liked, spoon a little Greek yogurt on top, or serve with fresh or dried fruit or chopped nuts. Drizzle or sprinkle over a little honey, agave syrup, maple syrup or brown sugar if you prefer your porridge sweetened.

COOK'S NOTES
- Only make two portions of porridge at a time as it needs plenty of room in the inner pot.
- It's important to release the pressure naturally; don't try to speed up the process by turning the pressure-release switch to the Venting position or the porridge may splatter out of the pressure valve.

Mixed Berry Quinoa Porridge

Frozen berries such as blueberries and raspberries are a great way to deliver a boost of vitamin C and antioxidants to your breakfast bowl, which is especially useful during the winter months when we tend to eat less fresh fruit. Like oats, quinoa contains soluble fibre, ideal for a sustaining breakfast to keep you satisfied for longer. It also helps reduce cholesterol levels.

SERVES 2

50g (2oz) quinoa flakes
25g (1oz) rolled oats
75g (3oz) frozen berries such as blueberries or mixed berries
450ml (¾ pint) milk, or almond or rice milk if you prefer
Honey, agave or maple syrup, to drizzle (optional)

1   Put the quinoa flakes and rolled oats in the inner pot. Scatter the frozen fruit over the top. Pour over the milk and stir gently.
2   Put on the lid and lock into place. Turn the pressure-release switch to Sealing. Press the Porridge button, adjust the pressure to High and the time to 3 minutes. After cooking, allow the pressure to release naturally (this will take 10–12 minutes).
3   Open the lid, stir the quinoa porridge and serve straight away, drizzled with honey, agave or maple syrup, if liked.

COOK'S NOTE
- Quinoa flakes are quinoa seeds that have been rolled in the same way as oat flakes. They have a slightly firmer texture than oats when cooked and are available in larger supermarkets and health-food stores.

Peach and Almond Couscous

Couscous can be used in both savoury and sweet dishes, such as this quick and easy hot cereal. You can use any type of milk you like, but almond milk works especially well with dried fruit such as peaches.

SERVES 2

75g (3oz) dried peaches (or other dried fruit, if preferred)
100g (4oz) couscous
Finely grated zest of ½ orange (optional)
450ml (¾ pint) almond milk, plus extra to serve
25g (1oz) toasted flaked almonds, to serve

1 Snip the dried peaches into small pieces, straight into the inner pot, using kitchen scissors. Add the couscous, and orange zest, if using. Pour over the milk and stir.

2 Put on the lid and lock into place. Turn the pressure-release switch to Sealing. Press the Manual (Pressure Cook) button, adjust the pressure to High and the time to 1 minute. After cooking, allow the pressure to release naturally (this will take 10–12 minutes).

3 Open the lid, stir, then divide between two bowls. Scatter with flaked almonds and serve with extra almond milk, if liked.

Boiled Eggs

(v)

If you've ever struggled to peel away the shell on a hot boiled egg, cooking them in your Instant Pot is a revelation, as the shell comes away quickly and easily without tearing bits of the egg white with it. Technically, cooking in your Instant Pot steams the eggs rather than boils them, but the results are the same. The timings here are for eggs straight from the fridge; if you cook them from room temperature, it will take a little less time for pressure to be reached.

SERVES 1-6

250ml (8fl oz) cold water
1–6 medium eggs

1   Place the trivet (steaming rack) in the inner pot and pour in the water. Place the eggs on the trivet, spacing them evenly.
2   Put on the lid and lock into place. Turn the pressure-release switch to Sealing. Press the Manual (Pressure Cook) button and adjust the pressure to High and the time: 3 minutes for soft boiled eggs, 4 minutes for medium, and 5 minutes for hard-boiled.
3   When cooking is complete, press the Keep Warm/Cancel button and quick-release the pressure. Remove the lid, lift the eggs out using tongs or a slotted spoon and serve straight away.

COOK'S NOTES

- If you are serving hard-boiled eggs cold or using them in a recipe, plunge them into a bowl of cold water (preferably with a few ice-cubes added) and leave to cool for 5 minutes before shelling. This prevents a grey tinge from forming around the outside of the egg yolk. Shelled hard-boiled eggs can be stored in the fridge, loosely wrapped in cling film, for 1–2 days. If you want to use them as a sandwich filling, it is better to make up the mixture with the freshly cooked eggs, then store in the fridge in a well-sealed container.

- To shell hard-boiled eggs: Crack the cooled egg all over with a teaspoon or tap it gently on a work surface. Start peeling off the shell at the rounded end, where there should be a gap under the shell from the air sac. Peel off the shell and its underlying membrane together. If necessary, rinse off any tiny bits of shell under cold running water.

Egg and Sausage Brunch

This recipe is based on traditional Scotch eggs, which are coated in breadcrumbs and deep-fried. This is a healthier version, with the sausage wrapping browned in a little oil, then steamed in your Instant Pot. If you have a non-stick inner pot, use it to fry the sausage-meat-coated eggs.

SERVES 2–4

250ml (8fl oz) cold water
4 small or medium eggs
15–30ml (1–2 tbsp) plain flour
400g (14oz) lean sausage meat
30ml (2 tbsp) chopped fresh parsley or 5ml (1 tsp) dried
   herbs such as sage and thyme
2.5ml (½ tsp) English mustard powder (optional)
Salt and freshly ground black pepper
15ml (1 tbsp) sunflower oil

1   Place the trivet (steaming rack) in the inner pot and pour in the water. Place the eggs on the trivet, spacing them evenly. Put on the lid and lock into place. Turn the pressure-release switch to Sealing. Press the Manual (Pressure Cook) button and adjust the pressure to High and the time to 4 minutes.

2   When cooking is complete, press the Keep Warm/Cancel button and allow the pressure to release naturally for 5 minutes, then quick-release any remaining pressure. Remove the lid, lift the eggs out using tongs or a slotted spoon and place in a bowl of cold water. Leave for 3–4 minutes, then shell the eggs, rinse under cold running water and pat dry on kitchen paper. Lightly dust with a little of the flour.

3 While the eggs are cooking, put the sausage meat in a bowl with the herbs, mustard powder, if using, salt and pepper. Mix well, divide into four equal balls, then pat out one of the pieces of sausage meat thinly to cover one hand (dust your hands first with flour to stop it sticking). Place one of the eggs on the flattened meat, then mould around the egg, squeezing and patting, so that it is an even thickness. Repeat with the remaining sausage meat and eggs.

4 Heat the oil in a non-stick frying pan and fry the sausage meatballs for 4–5 minutes, until lightly browned on all sides. Alternatively, remove the trivet (steaming rack) from your Instant Pot, tip out the water and wipe dry. Preheat your Instant Pot by pressing Sauté and adjust to More for a high heat. When the inner pot is hot, add the oil, then, after a few seconds, add the sausage meatballs and brown all over, turning carefully with a non-stick spatula, as they do tend to stick. Cancel the Sauté setting and remove the sausage balls from the pot.

5 If you've browned the sausage meatballs in your Instant Pot, return the trivet (steaming rack) to the inner pot and pour in 250ml (8fl oz) water (there's no need to wash the pot first). Carefully place the sausage meatballs on top of the trivet.

6 Put on the lid and lock into place. Turn the pressure-release switch to Sealing. Press the Manual (Pressure Cook) button and adjust the pressure to High and the time to 6 minutes. When the timer bleeps, press the Keep Warm/Cancel button and quick-release the pressure. Carefully remove the Scotch eggs, cut each in half and serve straight away, allowing either two or four halves per person.

COOK'S NOTES
- If you can't find good-quality lean sausage meat, simply buy your favourite sausages and remove the meat filling from the casings.
- Make sure you seal the edges of the sausage meat together when making the Scotch eggs, so that they don't split open during cooking.

Pancetta and Sun-dried Tomato Frittata

A frittata is a thick Italian omelette which is cooked until firm enough to be cut into wedges. Here it is made with crispy-cooked pancetta and full-flavoured sun-dried tomatoes. Although hash browns are a far cry from the Italian origins of this dish, they add to the taste and texture and turn this into a substantial breakfast.

SERVES 4

6 sun-dried tomatoes
4 rashers pancetta or smoked streaky bacon, chopped
200g (7oz) frozen hash browns
500ml (16fl oz) water
6 medium eggs
60ml (4 tbsp) milk
25g (1oz) freshly grated Parmesan cheese
Freshly ground black pepper

1   Put the tomatoes in a small heatproof bowl and pour over just enough boiling water to cover. Leave to soak while you prepare the remaining ingredients. Grease a 20cm (8in) round fixed-base non-stick cake tin and line with baking parchment.

2   Preheat the inner pot by selecting Sauté and adjust to More for a high heat. After 2 minutes, add the pancetta and cook for 2–3 minutes until sizzling and beginning to colour. Add the hash browns and stir for 2–3 minutes until almost thawed, breaking them up into smaller pieces. Press the Keep Warm/Cancel button to turn off the Sauté function.

3 Tip the pancetta and hash brown mixture into the prepared tin. Place the trivet (steaming rack) in the inner pot (don't unfold the handles or the cake tin won't fit) and pour in the water.

4 Drain the soaked tomatoes, finely chop and scatter over the pancetta and hash brown mixture in the tin. Whisk the eggs, milk, cheese and black pepper together, pour into the tin and place on the trivet (steaming rack).

5 Put on the lid and lock into place. Turn the pressure-release switch to Sealing. Press the Manual (Pressure Cook) button and adjust the pressure to High and the time to 12 minutes.

6 After cooking, quick-release the pressure. Unlock and remove the lid. Remove the tin from your Instant Pot. Carefully run a blunt knife around the edge of the frittata, turn out onto a board and remove the lining paper. Cut into wedges and serve hot.

Crispy Bacon and Red Onion Omelette

This is a cross between an omelette and a crustless quiche. Smoked bacon, tender onions and full-flavoured cheese are baked in a creamy savoury custard until lightly set. Hot buttered toast makes a great accompaniment.

SERVES 2

10g (2 tsp) unsalted butter, softened
3 rashers smoked streaky bacon, chopped
1 red onion, thinly sliced
75g (3oz) mature Cheddar, grated
250ml (8fl oz) water
3 medium eggs
100ml (4fl oz) milk
Freshly ground black pepper

1   Grease a 20cm (8in) round fixed-base non-stick cake tin with the butter. Preheat your Instant Pot by pressing Sauté and adjust to Normal for medium heat. Add the bacon and cook for about 3 minutes, stirring frequently, until crisp. Remove from the pot with a slotted spoon, leaving behind the fat released, and scatter the bacon in the base of the prepared tin.

2   Add the onion to your Instant Pot and cook for 3–4 minutes until soft. Add 15ml (1 tbsp) water if it starts to catch. Cancel the Sauté function. Remove the onion from the pot and add to the tin, spreading out evenly. Scatter the cheese over the top.

3   Carefully place the trivet (steaming rack) in your Instant Pot (don't unfold the handles or the tin won't fit), and pour in the water. There's no need to clean out the pot first: the steaming water will help do this as you cook the omelette.

4   Whisk together the eggs, milk and pepper. Pour into the tin over the bacon, onion and cheese. Cover the top with foil (this will stop condensation dripping onto the top of the omelette). Lower into your Instant Pot using a foil sling (see page 6).

5   Put on the lid and lock into place. Turn the pressure-release switch to Sealing. Press Manual (Pressure Cook), adjust the pressure to High and the time to 9 minutes. After cooking, allow the pressure to release naturally for 10 minutes, then quick-release any remaining pressure. Unlock and remove the lid.

6   Carefully lift out the omelette. Let it stand for a couple of minutes, then turn out and serve, cut into wedges.

VARIATION
- For a vegetarian version, make a Potato and Onion Omelette. Replace the bacon with 100g (4oz) cooked waxy new potatoes cut into small cubes. Grease the tin and preheat your Instant Pot, as in step 1 of main recipe, then add 15ml (1 tbsp) olive oil to the pot and when hot cook the onion for 3–4 minutes. Add the potatoes and stir for a further minute to coat in the oil, scatter in the prepared tin and continue as recipe from step 2.

Smoked Salmon and Avocado Kedgeree

Kedgeree was adapted from khichri, a rice and lentil dish, by British colonials on their return from India. Popular in Victorian times, it usually contains smoked haddock, but slivers of smoked salmon and avocado make a luxurious alternative.

SERVES 4

225g (8oz) white basmati rice
25g (1oz) unsalted butter
6 spring onions, trimmed and sliced
15ml (1 tbsp) korma curry paste
450ml (¾ pint) hot vegetable stock, preferably home-made
    (page 45)
Salt and freshly ground black pepper
1 large ripe avocado
10ml (2 tsp) lemon juice
50g (2oz) smoked salmon, cut into fine strips
30ml (2 tbsp) chopped fresh coriander
2 eggs, hard-boiled (page 18), peeled and cut lengthways into
    wedges
Wedges of lemon (optional), to serve

1   Rinse the rice in a sieve under cold running water. Put in a bowl, cover with plenty of cold water and leave to soak for a few minutes.
2   Preheat your Instant Pot by pressing Sauté and adjust to Normal for medium heat. Add the butter and when it has melted, add the spring onions and cook for 1 minute, stirring frequently, until beginning to soften. Stir in the curry paste and stir for a few more seconds. Add the drained rice, stock, salt and pepper and stir well. Cancel the Sauté function.

3 Put on the lid and lock into place. Turn the pressure-release switch to Sealing. Press Manual (Pressure Cook), adjust the pressure to High and the time to 4 minutes. After cooking, allow the pressure to release naturally for 5 minutes, then quick-release the remaining pressure.

4 While the rice is cooking, halve the avocado and remove the stone and peel. Cut into thin slices or chunks. Sprinkle the lemon juice over the avocado.

5 Unlock and remove the lid of your Instant Pot, then fork through the rice to separate the grains. Add the avocado, smoked salmon and coriander and mix well. Serve straight away, topped with hard-boiled egg wedges and, if liked, a quartered fresh lemon, to squeeze over.

Yogurt

Yogurt is simple to make in your Instant Pot, cheaper than shop-bought and can be made with the milk of your choice: full-fat, semi-skimmed or skimmed, depending on how rich you want it to be. Yogurt is made by culturing warmed pasteurised milk with lactic acid cultures (provided by a few spoonfuls of shop-bought yogurt), which turns the lactose in the milk to lactic acid and gives yogurt its classic tangy taste. The lactic acid alters the protein structure, giving yogurt its thick smooth texture.

Making yogurt in your Instant Pot involves two steps. The first is to pasteurise the milk by heating it to 82°C (180°F); this is done automatically by your Instant Pot and destroys any bacteria that might otherwise develop. The second step is to keep the milk warm at a constant temperature to allow the culture to work and turn the milk into yogurt.

MAKES ABOUT 600ML (1 PINT)

600ml (1 pint) milk
30ml (2 tbsp) plain 'live' yogurt (see Cook's notes, page 30)

1   Pour the milk into the inner pot. Put a lid on the yogurt, either a glass pan lid or your Instant Pot lid. Press the Yogurt button, then press Adjust until the display shows the word Boil. Leave until your Instant Pot bleeps; the display will then show the word Yogurt.
2   Remove the lid and leave until the milk has cooled to around 37°C (98°F). If you don't have a thermometer, dip your little finger (well-washed) into the milk; you should be able to comfortably keep it there for 5 seconds. You can speed up the cooling process by removing the inner pot and leaving it on a wire rack, or to cool even faster, place it in a sink of cold water.

3 When the milk has cooled enough, blend a little of the warm milk and yogurt together in a bowl, then whisk into the rest of the milk. Return the inner pot to your Instant Pot cooker (dry the outside of the bowl if you have cooled it in water). Put on a lid and press the Yogurt button. The display will show 8.00, which means 8 hours. There is no need to adjust the time, unless you want a very tangy yogurt (see Cook's notes). The display will then switch to 0.00 and will count up until it has reached 8 hours.

4 When your Instant Pot bleeps, remove the lid and carefully take out the inner pot. Leave to cool for about half an hour at room temperature. Cover the top with cling film and chill in the fridge for at least 4 hours, preferably overnight. The yogurt will set further and become thicker during this time.

COOK'S NOTES

- If you want a tangier yogurt, adjust the time to 10 hours in step 3. This will allow the lactic acid to develop a little more.
- For a creamier yogurt with a higher protein content, whisk 30–45ml (2–3 tbsp) powdered skimmed milk into the hot milk in step 2, after removing the lid and before leaving it to cool.
- You can use your home-made yogurt as a starter for the next batch of yogurt. To test if your shop-bought yogurt contains 'live' bacteria, blend 15ml (1 tbsp) yogurt with 75ml (5 tbsp) gently warmed milk in a small bowl. Leave in a warm place for at least 6 hours or overnight. If the mixture solidifies, there are live cultures present.
- Yogurt can be served plain or flavoured as you like (flavourings should always be added to the yogurt after it has been made, not during the process). Try fresh red berries, chopped tropical fruits, dried fruits soaked overnight in a little orange or apple juice, chopped nuts or unsweetened flaked coconut and simple spices such as pure vanilla extract or ground cinnamon.

VARIATIONS

- To make Greek yogurt, follow the recipe for yogurt, then pour it into a sieve lined with muslin and suspend over a bowl. Leave in the fridge for 4–6 hours; the liquid whey will slowly drip through into the bowl, leaving a firm, thicker yogurt in the sieve. You can use the whey in cooking (it's excellent instead of milk in soda bread or scones and will help them rise) or use instead of yogurt as a starter when making your next batch.

- Yogurt can also be used to make great smoothies. Quick and nourishing, these are ideal for breakfast time as they contain a good balance of protein, antioxidant vitamins, and minerals such as calcium, potassium and iron. Try one of the following:

- Breakfast Power Blend – Peel and slice 1 small ripe banana and put in a blender with a small handful of kale (optional), 50g (2oz) fresh or frozen blueberries, 5ml (1 tsp) wheatgerm, 100ml (4fl oz) chilled skimmed milk and 150ml (¼ pint) yogurt. Blend until smooth.

- Strawberry and Orange Yogurt Smoothie – Put 100g (4oz) fresh or frozen strawberries in a blender with the freshly squeezed juice of 1 orange. Add 75ml (5 tbsp) yogurt and 5ml (1 tsp) honey or agave syrup. Blend until smooth.

Individual Breakfast Bread and Custard Cups

(v)

Known in America as 'baked French toast', pieces of French bread (or ordinary white bread, if you prefer) are cooked in a sweet egg custard, flavoured with vanilla and cinnamon. Traditional versions are often enriched with cream and finished with a crumble topping, but this is a plainer, healthier dish. Make sure that your ramekins are heatproof and will fit side by side in your Instant Pot before you begin.

SERVES 4

150g (5oz) piece of day-old French stick
2 medium eggs
300ml (½ pint) milk
5ml (1 tsp) vanilla extract
2.5ml (½ tsp) ground cinnamon
5–10ml (1–2 tsp) soft light brown sugar
Pinch of salt (optional)
250ml (8fl oz) water
25g (1oz) unsalted butter, softened
Maple syrup, fruit compote or fresh berries, to serve (optional)

1   Tear the bread into small pieces or cut into cubes about 2cm (¾in). Place in a bowl.
2   Whisk the eggs, milk, vanilla, cinnamon, sugar and salt, if using, together in a jug, then pour over the bread. Leave to soak for a minute or two, then give the mixture a gentle stir.
3   Place the trivet (steaming rack) in the inner pot and pour in the water. Lightly grease the insides of four 150ml (¼ pint) ramekins with about half of the softened butter. Divide the soaked bread mixture between the ramekins. Cover the top of each with a piece of foil. Place the ramekins on the trivet.

4 Put on the lid and lock into place. Turn the pressure-release switch to Sealing. Select Steam and adjust the pressure to High and the time to 10 minutes.

5 When cooking is complete, press the Keep Warm/Cancel button and allow the pressure to release naturally for 5 minutes, then quick-release the remaining pressure. Unlock and lift off the lid. Carefully remove the ramekins using tongs and leave to cool for a few minutes. Run a knife around the edge of each ramekin, then turn out.

6 Melt the remaining butter in a non-stick frying pan. When hot, add the bread and custard cups and cook for about 2 minutes on each side until golden brown. Serve with a drizzle of maple syrup, fruit compote or fresh berries.

COOK'S NOTE
- Use a low-calorie cooking spray instead of the butter if preferred. If you don't want to brown them, finish with a light dusting of icing sugar.

Dried Apricot and Almond Conserve

The fresh apricot season is very short, but this glorious golden jam can be made and enjoyed at any time of the year. Dried fruit such as apricots are a good source of iron and antioxidants; almonds provide a protein boost to start your day.

MAKES ABOUT 1KG/2¼LB

350g (12oz) dried apricots
450ml (¾ pint) apple juice
Finely grated zest and juice of 1 lemon
350g (12oz) preserving sugar
50g (2oz) blanched almonds, chopped

1 Snip each apricot into quarters using clean kitchen scissors. Put them in the inner pot and pour over the apple juice. Cover the pot and leave to soak at room temperature for 1 hour (or overnight in the fridge, if you prefer).

2 Add the lemon zest and juice to the pot. Put on the lid and lock into place. Select Manual (Pressure Cook), adjust the pressure to High and the time to 5 minutes.

3 After cooking, quick-release the pressure. Add the sugar to the pot, press Sauté and adjust to Less for a low heat. Stir constantly until the sugar has dissolved, then press Keep Warm/Cancel. Press Sauté again, this time adjusting to More for a high heat.

4 Boil for 10–15 minutes, or until the jam is very thick, stirring frequently to prevent it catching on the bottom of the pot. After 10 minutes, spoon a little – no more than 2.5ml (½ tsp) onto a chilled plate. Leave for a minute, then push with your finger; if the top wrinkles a little, the jam has reached setting point. If not, cook for a few more minutes. Cancel the Sauté setting immediately the jam reaches the desired thickness, as it will continue to cook in the residual heat.

5 Stir the chopped almonds into the jam and leave to stand for 15 minutes, then ladle the jam into warmed sterilised jars (see Cook's notes). Seal, then leave to cool completely. Label and store in a cool dark place. Eat within a year of making.

COOK'S NOTES

- **Sterilising jars** It's essential to sterilise the jars if you want to keep the jam for more than a few weeks. Check jars for cracks or damage, then wash thoroughly in hot, soapy water, rinse well and turn upside down to drain. The simplest way to clean and sterilise is to put the jars and lids in a dishwasher and run it on its hottest setting, including drying.
- You can also sterilise the jars in the oven: Space the jars and lids slightly apart on a baking tray lined with kitchen paper. Place in a cold oven, then heat to 110°C/225°F/Gas mark ¼. Heat for 30 minutes, then turn off the oven. Fill the jars while still warm.

Winter Fruit Compote

There's no need to miss out on your 'five-a-day' during the colder months. This really simple fruit dish is great served warm, or you can make it in the evening and serve chilled the following day.

SERVES 4

500g (1¼lb) pack dried fruit salad
4 whole cloves
½ cinnamon stick
175ml (6fl oz) apple juice, preferably clear
Greek yogurt (page 30) or soya yogurt, to serve (optional)

1   Put the dried fruit, cloves and cinnamon stick in the inner pot. Pour over the apple juice.
2   Put on the lid and lock into place. Press Manual (Pressure Cook), adjust the pressure to High and the time to 2 minutes.
3   When cooking is complete, press Keep Warm/Cancel and allow the pressure to release naturally (this will take about 10 minutes).
4   Serve warm or leave to cool and then chill in the fridge. It will keep for up to 5 days.

COOK'S NOTE
- You can use a bag of dried fruit salad, which usually contains apricots, prunes and dried apples, or create your own favourite blend. Dried tropical fruit blends are also available, which often include mango, papaya and pineapple. These work well with orange or pineapple juice.

Lemon and Ginger Marmalade

If you are looking for a change from the usual orange marmalade, this tangy lemon version has the added kick of warm, spicy ginger. When making marmalade on the hob, it usually takes around 2 hours to tenderise the peel; here it is done in 10 minutes.

MAKES ABOUT 900G (2LB)

500g (1¼lb) lemons
75g (3oz) fresh ginger, peeled and finely grated
600ml (1 pint) water
450g (1lb) granulated sugar

1   Quarter and thinly slice the lemons. Reserve any pips and tie them in a muslin bag. Place the lemons and pip bag in your Instant Pot with the ginger and water.
2   Put on the lid and lock into place. Select Manual (Pressure Cook), adjust the pressure to High and the time to 10 minutes. After cooking, allow the pressure to release naturally for 10 minutes, then quick-release the remaining pressure.
3   Unlock and remove the lid. Remove the muslin pip bag and squeeze the juices into the pan to release the pectin (either wait until cool enough to handle or wear clean rubber gloves).
4   Add the sugar to the pot and stir well. Select Sauté and adjust to Less for low heat. Stir until the sugar has completely dissolved. Press Keep Warm/Cancel, then press Sauté again and adjust to More for high heat. Boil for 15–20 minutes, or until setting point is reached: 105°C (220°F) on a sugar thermometer. Turn off your Instant Pot.
5   Skim any scum from the surface using a wooden spoon. Leave to cool for 5 minutes, stir to distribute the peel, then ladle into warmed sterilised jars (see page 35) and seal. When cold, label and store in a cool place. Use within a year of making.

2

Soups, Stocks and Broths

Your Instant Pot truly excels when it comes to soup making. Full of healthy ingredients, soups fit the bill for everyday meals and special menus throughout the year. Here you'll discover elegant soups such as Italian Vegetable Soup and Chilled Avocado Soup and warming one-bowl lunch and supper dishes including Tagine-style Lamb Soup and Barley Broth with Chicken.

A good stock is essential for soup and casserole making. Bone broth, chicken stock and vegetable stock are all packed with micronutrients and are incredibly quick and easy to make in your Instant Pot. Fresh stock should be covered and kept in the fridge as soon as it is cool, then used within 3 days of making. If you are not planning to use it within this time, freeze in small quantities and don't forget to label. Note that commercial stock cubes often contain a lot of salt, so if you are not using home-made stock in recipes, it is better to season dishes after cooking.

Bone Broth

A good stock is the basis of many soups and meat dishes and before the invention of stock cubes and powder, it was usual to have a bubbling stockpot in the kitchen, extracting the last of the flavour and nutrients from leftover bones. Bone broth is now in vogue, with many perceived health benefits. Luckily, there's no need to have a pan boiling away for hours on the hob – bone broth can be made easily and much more quickly in your Instant Pot.

MAKES ABOUT 2 LITRES (3½ PINTS)

2kg (4½lb) beef bones or lamb bones
Raw leftover onion ends, carrot peelings or celery ends (up to 2 handfuls)
6 black peppercorns
2 bay leaves
15ml (1 tbsp) cider vinegar or lemon juice
Cold water, preferably filtered

1 Put the bones and vegetable leftovers in the inner pot, packing tightly; the pot should be no more than half-full. Add the peppercorns, tuck in the bay leaves and sprinkle over the vinegar or lemon juice.
2 Pour over enough water to cover the bones by about 5cm (2in), but make sure the water doesn't come above the 4-litre (7-pint) mark in the inner pot.
3 Put on the lid and lock into place. Select Manual (Pressure Cook), adjust the pressure to High and the time to 1 hour, 30 minutes. After cooking, allow the pressure to release naturally. Unlock and remove the lid.

4 Strain the stock through a fine mesh strainer into a clean bowl and leave to cool. If you aren't using straight away, cover and chill in the fridge. A layer of fat will come to the surface, which you should remove. Use within 3 days of making, or freeze when cool.

COOK'S NOTES
- Many butchers are happy to give you bones for free or for a nominal amount and will often chop them into smaller pieces for you if you ask.
- Whenever you prepare vegetables, pop the ends and peelings (wash carrots before peeling) into a bag and freeze ready for broth/stock-making.
- Beef bones produce a lot of fat, which is excellent for frying and roasting.
- Adding a dash of cider vinegar or lemon juice will help to extract minerals from the meat bones.

Brown Beef Stock

This rich stock can be used as the base for clear soups such as beef consommé and French onion soup, and adds depth to the colour and flavour of casseroles, stews and gravies. The bones and vegetables are lightly roasted in the oven first. This stock is cooked using the Slow Cook function as rapid cooking may make it cloudy.

MAKES ABOUT 1.5 LITRES (2½ PINTS)

900g (2lb) beef or veal bones
1 onion, unpeeled and quartered
1 carrot, sliced
1 stick celery, sliced
2 bay leaves
6 black peppercorns
About 1.5 litres (2½ pints) cold water, preferably filtered

1   Preheat the oven to 220°C/425°F/Gas mark 7. Using a meat cleaver, chop up any large bones into smaller pieces (or ask your butcher to do this for you). Place in a large, heavy roasting tin. Roast for 15 minutes, turning several times during cooking.
2   Add the onion, carrot and celery. Return to the oven and roast for a further 10–15 minutes, or until the bones are well browned and the vegetables tinged with brown at the edges.
3   Transfer the bones and vegetables to the inner pot, packing them tightly and tucking in the bay leaves and peppercorns. Pour over enough cold water to cover by about 2.5cm (1in) and coming no higher than the 4-litre (7-pint) mark in the inner pot.

4 Put on the lid, lock into place, select Slow Cook and adjust to More for a high heat. Cook for 2 hours. When the cooking time is up, press Cancel, remove the lid and skim off any scum. Lock the lid into place again, select Slow Cook and adjust to Normal for a medium heat, and the time to 4 hours.

5 After cooking, remove the lid and strain the stock through a fine sieve into a bowl. Cool by placing the bowl in a sink of cold water, then cover and chill in the fridge. Remove the fat from the surface of the stock. Use within 3 days of making, or freeze when cool.

Golden Chicken Stock

This simple stock can be made using a fresh or cooked chicken carcass, poultry bones or chicken wings. It's perfect for soups, chicken casseroles or white sauces. Onion skins add little flavour to the stock but will give it a rich golden colour.

MAKES ABOUT 1 LITRE (1¾ PINTS)

1 fresh or cooked chicken carcass
1 onion, unpeeled and quartered
1 carrot, sliced
1 stick celery, sliced
2 bay leaves
1 sprig fresh thyme (optional)
6 white peppercorns
About 1 litre (1¾ pints) cold water, preferably filtered

1 Use poultry shears to cut the chicken carcass into smaller pieces and pack into the inner pot with the onion, carrot, celery, bay leaves, thyme, if using, and peppercorns. Pour over the water.

2 Put on the lid, lock into place and turn the pressure-release switch to Sealing. Select Manual (Pressure Cook) and adjust the pressure to High and the time to 1 hour.

3 After cooking, allow the pressure to release naturally. Remove the lid and strain the stock through a fine sieve into a bowl. Cool by placing the bowl in a sink of cold water, then cover and chill. Remove the fat from the surface of the stock. Use within 3 days of making, or freeze when cool.

COOK'S NOTE

• For extra flavour, cook two or three chicken carcasses at the same time. Roughly chop them and store in the freezer until you are ready to make stock. There's no need to add extra vegetables or herbs for the extra bones. Add just enough water to cover the bones, but don't fill the inner pot higher than the 4-litre mark.

Vegetable Stock

You can vary the vegetables in the stock and use more or less of any type, depending on what you have available. It's a good idea to freeze leftover peelings such as carrots (wash them well before peeling), leek and onion ends and save them for stock-making. Avoid large quantities of strong-tasting vegetables such as turnips and parsnips as their flavour will dominate, or potatoes, which would make the stock cloudy.

MAKES ABOUT 1 LITRE (1¾ PINTS)

1 large onion, unpeeled and roughly chopped
1 leek, roughly chopped
2 carrots, sliced
1 stick celery, sliced
2 bay leaves
1 sprig fresh thyme (optional)
A few fresh parsley stalks (optional)
6 white peppercorns
About 1 litre (1¾ pints) cold water, preferably filtered

1   Pack the vegetables into the inner pot, tucking the bay leaves, thyme and parsley stalks in the middle. Scatter over the peppercorns and pour in enough water to come about 2cm (¾in) above the vegetables.
2   Put on the lid and lock into place. Turn the pressure-release switch to Sealing. Select Manual (Pressure Cook), adjust the pressure to High and the time to 30 minutes.
3   After cooking, allow the pressure to release naturally. Remove the lid and strain the stock through a sieve into a bowl. Leave to cool, then cover and chill in the fridge. Use within 5 days of making, or freeze when cool.

Fiery Fresh Tomato and Basil Soup

v

Serve this vibrant soup in late summer when fresh tomatoes are full of flavour and inexpensive. Make it as spicy or as mild as you like by increasing or reducing the number of chillies.

SERVES 4

15ml (1 tbsp) olive oil
15g (½oz) butter
1 red onion, chopped
2 cloves garlic, roughly chopped
1-2 red chillies, halved, seeded and chopped
900g (2lb) ripe tomatoes, skinned and roughly chopped
600ml (1 pint) vegetable stock, preferably home-made
   (page 45)
100ml (4fl oz) dry white wine or extra vegetable stock
15ml (1 tbsp) sun-dried tomato purée
Salt and freshly ground black pepper
45ml (3 tbsp) shredded fresh basil
Whole basil leaves, to garnish

1 Preheat your Instant Pot by selecting Sauté and adjust to Normal for medium heat. When the inner pot is hot, add the olive oil and butter and heat until the butter has melted. Add the red onion and cook, stirring frequently, for 4–5 minutes, until beginning to soften.
2 Add the garlic and chillies and stir for a further minute, then add the tomatoes, stock, wine or extra stock and the tomato purée. Stir well, then cancel the Sauté setting. Put on the lid and lock into place.

3 Select Soup setting, adjust the pressure to High and the time to 6 minutes. When the cooking is complete, allow the pressure to release naturally for 10 minutes, then quick-release any remaining pressure. Unlock and remove the lid.

4 Use a hand-held blender to purée the soup to a smooth consistency (or purée in a jug blender). Season with salt and pepper to taste, then stir in the shredded basil. Ladle into warmed bowls and serve garnished with basil leaves.

COOK'S NOTES
- Skin the tomatoes by putting them in a heatproof bowl. Pour over enough boiling water to cover and leave for a minute, then drain. When cool enough to handle, the skins should peel off easily.
- Shred the basil at the last minute as it loses freshness quickly when cut.
- When fresh tomatoes aren't in season, make this with 2 x 400g (14oz) cans of chopped tomatoes.

Tex-Mex Bean Soup with Guacamole Salsa

Dried beans are so much cheaper than buying the canned version and quick and easy to cook in your Instant Pot. This spicy soup is served with a cooling avocado and lime-juice salsa, but for a simpler finish, add a swirl of Greek yogurt instead.

SERVES 4

15ml (1 tbsp) salt
125g (4½oz) dried red kidney beans
15ml (1 tbsp) olive oil
1 red onion, chopped
1 clove garlic, crushed
2.5ml (½ tsp) ground cumin
2.5ml (½ tsp) ground coriander
2.5ml (½ tsp) chilli powder
5ml (1 tsp) smoked paprika
450ml (¾ pint) vegetable stock, preferably home-made (page 45)
450ml (¾ pint) tomato juice
Freshly ground black pepper

For the guacamole salsa
1 small red onion, very finely chopped
Juice of 1 lime
1 large ripe avocado
30ml (2 tbsp) chopped fresh coriander

1 Dissolve the salt in a large bowl of cold water. Add the dried beans and leave to soak for at least 8 hours. Drain and rinse, then drain again.

2 Preheat your Instant Pot by selecting Sauté and adjust to Normal for medium heat. Add the oil and when hot, add the onion. Cook for 3–4 minutes, stirring frequently. Add a spoonful of stock if the onion starts to stick. Add the garlic and spices. Stir in the drained beans, stock and tomato juice and lightly season with black pepper.

3 Put on the lid and lock into place. Press Soup, adjust the pressure to High and the time to 20 minutes. After cooking, allow the pressure to release naturally for 10 minutes, then quick-release any remaining pressure. Unlock and remove the lid. Select Sauté and adjust to Normal for medium heat, to keep the soup hot.

4 While the soup cooks, prepare the salsa: Mix the onion and lime juice in a small bowl. Leave to stand for 10 minutes (this will soften the flavour of the onion). Halve, stone and peel the avocado, then dice finely. Add to the onion with the chopped coriander and mix well.

5 Ladle about two-thirds of the soup into a blender or food processor and process until smooth. Pour back into your Instant Pot and stir well. Taste and adjust the seasoning if necessary.

6 Ladle the soup into warmed bowls. Spoon a little guacamole salsa into the middle of each and serve straight away.

Wild Mushroom Soup

This is a rich autumnal soup with the mushroom flavours enhanced with dried mushrooms and enlivened with a dash of Madeira. Serve it with chunks of warm rustic-style white or wholemeal bread.

SERVES 4

15g (½oz) dried wild mushrooms, such as morels or porcini
600ml (1 pint) hot chicken or vegetable stock, preferably
   home-made (pages 44–45)
15g (½oz) unsalted butter
15ml (1 tbsp) sunflower oil
1 onion, finely chopped
2 cloves garlic, crushed
450g (1lb) button mushrooms, sliced
15ml (1 tbsp) plain flour
2.5ml (½ tsp) dried thyme
45ml (3 tbsp) Madeira or dry sherry
Salt and freshly ground black pepper
60ml (4 tbsp) half-fat crème fraiche, to serve

1 Put the dried mushrooms in a heatproof bowl and cover with cold water, then rinse well in a sieve to remove any grit. Return to the bowl and pour over the stock. Leave to soak for a few minutes while you prepare the other ingredients.
2 Preheat your Instant Pot by selecting Sauté and adjust to Normal for medium heat. Add the butter and oil and when the butter has melted, add the onion and cook for 2–3 minutes, stirring frequently. Add the garlic and button mushrooms and continue to sauté for 4–5 minutes, stirring frequently, until softened. Add a tablespoon of the stock if they start to stick to the pan. Cancel the Sauté function.

3 Sprinkle the flour over the onion and mushrooms and stir well. Stir in the thyme and Madeira or sherry, then add the soaked mushrooms and stock and season with salt and pepper.

4 Put on the lid and lock into place. Select Manual (Pressure Cook), adjust the pressure to High and the time to 10 minutes. After cooking, allow the pressure to release naturally for 10 minutes, then quick-release any remaining pressure. Unlock and remove the lid.

5 Use a hand-held blender to purée the soup until smooth or purée in a jug blender, then reheat on the Sauté and More settings for 5 minutes. Ladle into warmed bowls, and swirl a little crème fraiche on the top of each before serving.

Butternut Squash Soup

This gorgeous golden soup is spiced with a little fresh ginger, which adds a warm and fresh flavour. You can also make it with scooped-out pumpkin flesh, left over from making Hallowe'en lanterns. A scattering of toasted pumpkin seeds adds a crunchy texture.

SERVES 4

45ml (3 tbsp) pumpkin seeds
30ml (2 tbsp) sunflower oil
1 onion, chopped
2.5cm (1in) piece fresh ginger, peeled and grated
1.5ml (¼ tsp) ground turmeric
1 butternut squash, about 1kg (2¼lb), halved, seeded, peeled
    and roughly chopped
600ml (1 pint) vegetable stock, preferably home-made
    (page 45)
Salt and freshly ground black pepper

1   Select Sauté and adjust to Normal for medium heat. Add the pumpkin seeds to the inner pot and toast for 3–4 minutes, stirring frequently, until the skins start to split and they smell nutty. Remove from the pot with a spoon and set aside.
2   Add the oil to the inner pot, then add the onion and cook for 3–4 minutes or until beginning to soften. Add the ginger and turmeric and cook for a further minute, then add the butternut squash and vegetable stock. Season with salt and pepper. Cancel the Sauté function.
3   Put on the lid and lock into place. Select Manual (Pressure Cook), adjust the pressure to High and the time to 10 minutes. After cooking, allow the pressure to release naturally for 10 minutes, then quick-release the remaining pressure. Unlock and remove the lid.

4 Use a hand-held blender to purée the soup until very smooth (or purée in a jug blender, then reheat for a few minutes using the Sauté function, adjusted to More for high heat). Add a little more hot vegetable stock if you prefer a thinner consistency. Taste and adjust the seasoning, if needed. Ladle into warmed bowls and scatter with toasted pumpkin seeds before serving.

COOK'S NOTE
- Butternut squash can be tough to peel. To tenderise the skin, prick in several places with a fork and microwave on high for 3 minutes. Leave until cool enough to handle before peeling.

VARIATION
- For Pumpkin Soup, substitute pumpkin flesh for the butternut squash and make in exactly the same way. You will need less stock, around 550ml (18fl oz), as pumpkins have a slightly higher water content.

Chorizo and Chickpea Soup

This lightly spiced soup is robust and satisfying and is a great meal on a cold day. Serve with crusty wholemeal bread or wedges of warm cornbread (page 226).

SERVES 4

Pinch of saffron strands
10ml (2 tsp) olive oil
225g (8oz) chorizo sausage, cut into 1cm (½in) cubes
350g (12oz) new potatoes, scrubbed and quartered
400g (14oz) can chickpeas, rinsed and drained, or 250g (9oz) cooked chickpeas (page 8)
400g (14oz) can chopped tomatoes
350ml (12fl oz) vegetable stock, preferably home-made (page 45)
1 bay leaf
Salt and freshly ground black pepper
45ml (3 tbsp) chopped fresh parsley

1 Put the saffron in a small bowl and pour over 15ml (1 tbsp) hot water. Leave to soak. Preheat your Instant Pot by pressing Sauté and adjust to Normal for a medium heat. When the pot is hot, add the oil, then the chorizo. Cook for about 4 minutes, stirring frequently, until lightly browned. Remove from the pot using a slotted spoon, leaving the oil behind.

2 Add the potatoes and cook for a minute, stirring all the time, until they are coated in the oil. Add the chickpeas, tomatoes, stock, soaked saffron and liquid and the bay leaf. Season with salt and pepper. Cancel the Sauté function.

3 Put on the lid and lock into place. Press Manual (Pressure Cook), adjust the pressure to High and the time to 5 minutes. After cooking is complete, allow the pressure to release naturally for 10 minutes, then quick-release the remaining pressure.

4 Unlock and remove the lid. Stir the chopped parsley into the soup and adjust the seasoning if needed. Ladle into warmed soup bowls and serve straight away.

Lentil and Leftovers Soup

This is so much nicer than it sounds and is a great way to use up all those bits and pieces of vegetables in your fridge, including broccoli stalks and the ends of asparagus that are usually thrown away. It doesn't matter if some of the vegetables are a bit tough and stringy, as the soup is sieved after puréeing to make it super-smooth.

SERVES 4

100g (4oz) red lentils
350g (12oz) raw vegetables such as leek, carrot, courgette, butternut squash, broccoli stalks, asparagus stems, cauliflower leaves (only use the fresh green ones and remove tough stalks)
1 bay leaf
750–900ml (1¼–1½ pints) well-flavoured vegetable stock, preferably home-made (page 45)
Salt and freshly ground black pepper

1 Rinse the lentils in a sieve under cold running water. Drain well, then tip them into your Instant Pot. Roughly chop the vegetables into smallish similar-sized pieces and add to the pot with the bay leaf. Pour in 750ml (1¼ pints) of the stock and season with salt and pepper.

2 Put on the lid, lock into place and turn the pressure-release switch to Sealing. Press Manual (Pressure Cook), adjust the pressure to High and adjust the time to 6 minutes.

3 After cooking, allow the pressure to release naturally. Unlock and remove the lid and discard the bay leaf. Purée the soup using a hand-held blender or in a jug blender. If some of the vegetables you have used were slightly stringy, pass the soup through a fine stainless-steel or plastic sieve to remove them.

4 The soup should still be piping hot, but if necessary, reheat in your rinsed-out Instant Pot by selecting Sauté and adjusting to More for a high heat. Ladle into warmed bowls and serve straight away.

COOK'S NOTE
- If you use mostly high-water vegetables, such as courgettes or butternut squash, use a little less stock. You can adjust the consistency of the soup after making by adding more of the stock or milk (non-dairy milk if you are vegan) if you prefer.

Tagine-style Lamb Soup

This is a cross between a soup and a stew and can be served as a main meal. A tagine is a conical ceramic pot in which this dish is traditionally cooked; your Instant Pot will do the job just as well!

SERVES 4

30ml (2 tbsp) olive oil
400g (14oz) lamb fillet, trimmed and cut into small cubes
1 onion, chopped
2 cloves garlic, crushed
30ml (2 tbsp) ras-el-hanout spice mix
10ml (2 tsp) plain flour
900ml (1½ pints) hot vegetable stock, preferably home-made (page 45)
400g (14oz) can chopped tomatoes
50g (2oz) dried apricots, quartered
1 stick celery, chopped
450g (1lb) butternut squash, peeled, seeded and cut into 2cm (¾in) cubes
Salt and freshly ground black pepper

For the couscous
200ml (7fl oz) boiling vegetable stock, preferably home-made (page 45)
100g (4oz) couscous
30ml (2 tbsp) chopped fresh mint

1   Preheat your Instant Pot by selecting Sauté and adjust to More for high heat. Add 15ml (1 tbsp) of the oil. Pat the lamb dry on kitchen paper, add to the pot and fry for 3–4 minutes until browned all over. Remove and set aside. Cancel the Sauté setting.

2   Select Sauté again, but this time adjust to Normal for medium heat. Add the remaining 15ml (1 tbsp) oil, then add the onion and cook for 3–4 minutes, stirring frequently, until almost soft. Add the garlic and ras-el-hanout spice mix and stir for a further minute. Add a couple of teaspoonfuls of stock if the mixture starts to stick. Sprinkle over the flour and stir, then gradually add the stock.

3   Cancel the Sauté setting, then add the chopped tomatoes, apricots, celery and butternut squash. Return the lamb and any juices to the pot and season with salt and pepper. Stir everything together.

4   Put on the lid and lock into place. Select Manual (Pressure Cook), turn the pressure-release switch to Sealing and adjust the pressure to High and the time to 15 minutes. After cooking, allow the pressure to release naturally for 10 minutes, then quick-release the remaining pressure. Unlock and remove the lid.

5   While the pressure releases naturally, prepare the couscous: Pour the boiling stock into a heatproof bowl and pour in the couscous. Stir, then cover the bowl with a pan lid and leave to stand for 5 minutes. Stir in the chopped mint using a fork (this will help to separate the grains).

6   Ladle the soup into warmed bowls and pile the couscous into the middle of each. Serve straight away.

COOK'S NOTES
- To make a more substantial meal, add 200g (7oz) cooked chickpeas to the tagine in step 3.
- For an attractive finish, scatter about 125g (4½oz) prepared pomegranate seeds over the soup before serving.

Chicken Tinola

This Filipino soup is traditionally made with a whole chicken, simmered for a long time to extract all the flavour from the meat and bones. Here, inexpensive chicken thighs are used, which your Instant Pot cooks in minutes rather than hours. Sliced green mangoes or chayotes are often added to the soup, but courgettes are an easier-to-find alternative.

SERVES 4

6 skinless chicken thighs
1 litre (1¾ pints) chicken stock, preferably home-made
   (page 44)
2.5cm (1in) piece fresh ginger, roughly chopped
2 cloves garlic, peeled
2 medium carrots
1 bunch (about 8) spring onions, shredded
200g (7oz) pak choi (bok choy) or choi sum, trimmed
2 medium courgettes, sliced

1   Remove any bits of fat from the chicken thighs, rinse under cold water and place in the inner pot. Add the stock, ginger and garlic. Scrub the carrots and then peel them, retaining the peel. Trim the green stalks and root ends from the spring onions and add these trimmings and the carrot peelings to the pot (keep the white parts for later).

2   Put on the lid and lock into place. Press Manual (Pressure Cook), turn the pressure-release switch to Sealing and adjust the pressure to High and the time to 12 minutes. After cooking, allow the pressure to release naturally for 10 minutes, then quick-release any remaining pressure. Unlock and remove the lid.

3   Tip the chicken and stock into a large sieve over a bowl. Remove the chicken and place on a board, retaining the stock. Discard the ginger, garlic, carrot and onion trimmings. When cool enough, remove the chicken from the bones and cut into bite-sized pieces. Skim any fat from the stock.

4   Halve the carrots lengthways and thinly slice. Shred the pak choi leaves and thinly slice the pak choi stalks. Add the carrots, pak choi, spring onions and courgettes to your Instant Pot along with the chicken pieces. Pour over the stock.

5   Put on the lid and lock into place. Press Manual (Pressure Cook), turn the pressure-release switch to Sealing and adjust pressure to High and the time to 2 minutes. After cooking, quick-release the pressure. Unlock and remove the lid. Ladle the soup into warmed bowls and serve straight away.

COOK'S NOTE
- Choi sum is leafier and darker green than pak choi and has a subtle mustard flavour. It is available in many large supermarkets.

Barley Broth with Chicken

Barley is regaining popularity, not only because it is a tasty and versatile grain but because it is also rich in nutrients, in particular vitamin B6, potassium and iron.

SERVES 4

40g (1½oz) pearl barley
15ml (1 tbsp) sunflower oil
1 onion, finely chopped
1 carrot, finely chopped
1 stick celery, finely chopped
1 leek, trimmed, halved lengthways and finely sliced
1 small potato, about 100g (4oz), peeled and cut into 1cm
    (½in) dice
4 chicken drumsticks, skinned
1 bay leaf
1 litre (1¾ pints) chicken stock, preferably home-made
    (page 44)
Salt and freshly ground black pepper
45ml (3 tbsp) chopped fresh parsley

1   Rinse the pearl barley in a sieve under cold running water.
    Tip into a small bowl, cover with cold water and leave to soak
    for a few minutes.
2   Preheat your Instant Pot by selecting Sauté and adjust to
    Normal for medium heat. Add the oil and let it heat for a
    minute, then add the onion. Cook for 3–4 minutes, stirring
    frequently, until almost soft, then stir in the carrot, celery
    and leek. Cook for a further minute.

3 Cancel the Sauté function. Drain the pearl barley and add to the pot with the potato. Stir, then add the chicken drumsticks and bay leaf. Pour over the stock and season with salt and pepper.

4 Put on the lid and lock into place. Press Poultry, turn the pressure-release switch to Sealing and adjust the pressure to High. The time should automatically set to 15 minutes. After cooking, quick-release the pressure. Unlock and remove the lid.

5 Remove the chicken drumsticks and take the meat off the bones. Chop into bite-sized pieces (cover the soup with the lid while you do this to keep it hot). Stir the chicken and parsley into the soup. Ladle the soup into warmed bowls and serve straight away.

COOK'S NOTE
- Use 'pearl' rather than 'pot' barley for this recipe. Although it is slightly less nutritious because it is more refined, it is more easily digested and some of the starch in the grains will be released into the soup and act as a thickener.

Goulash Soup with Mini Bread Dumplings

This main-meal slow-cooked soup, seasoned with smoked paprika, originates in Hungary. It is topped with light little dumplings made from breadcrumbs and traditionally flavoured with caraway seeds.

SERVES 4

15ml (1 tbsp) sunflower oil
1 onion, finely chopped
450g (1lb) lean braising steak, trimmed and cut into 1cm (½in) cubes
10ml (2 tsp) smoked paprika, plus extra for sprinkling
100g (4oz) white cabbage, finely shredded
2 medium carrots, peeled, halved lengthways and thickly sliced
350ml (12fl oz) hot bone broth or beef stock, preferably home-made (page 40)
400g (14oz) can chopped tomatoes
Salt and freshly ground black pepper

For the dumplings
1 medium egg
15ml (1 tbsp) milk
75g (3oz) fresh white breadcrumbs
15ml (1 tbsp) chopped fresh parsley
1.5ml (¼ tsp) caraway seeds (optional)
Crème fraiche or sour cream, to serve

1   Preheat the inner pot by selecting Sauté and adjust to Normal for medium heat. Add the oil and let it heat for a minute, then add the onion and cook for 3–4 minutes, stirring frequently. Cancel the Sauté function.

2   Toss the braising steak in the paprika and add to your Instant Pot along with the cabbage and carrots. Pour over the broth or stock and the chopped tomatoes. Season with salt and pepper and stir well.

3   Put on the lid and lock into place. Turn the pressure-release switch to Venting. Press Slow Cook and adjust to More for a high heat; the time will automatically set to 4 hours.

4   When cooking is complete, press Cancel. Unlock and remove the lid and stir the soup, then press Sauté and adjust to Less for a low heat. Cover the soup with a pan lid. Leave for 5 minutes or until boiling.

5   Meanwhile, make the dumplings. Beat the egg and milk together in a bowl with a little salt and pepper. Add the breadcrumbs, parsley and caraway seeds, if using. Mix well, then with damp hands, shape into 12 small balls.

6   Carefully place the dumplings on top of the boiling soup. Re-cover with the lid and cook for 15 minutes. Serve straight away, topped with a little crème fraiche or sour cream and a sprinkling of paprika.

Creamy Pear and Roquefort Soup

Blue cheese and pears is a classic combination and this rich and smooth soup makes the perfect dinner-party starter, especially when pears are at their best during the still-warm days and cooler evenings at the beginning of autumn.

SERVES 4

15ml (½oz) unsalted butter
1 onion, finely chopped
3 medium-sized ripe pears, peeled, cored and chopped
400ml (14fl oz) vegetable stock, preferably home-made
(page 45)
15ml (1 tbsp) lemon juice
200g (7oz) Roquefort cheese, crumbled
Freshly ground black pepper

1   Preheat your Instant Pot by selecting Sauté and adjust to Normal for medium heat. Add the butter and when it has melted add the onion. Cook for 3–4 minutes, stirring frequently, until almost soft.

2   Cancel the Sauté function and add the pears and stock to the pot. Put on the lid and lock into place. Turn the pressure valve to Sealing. Press Manual (Pressure Cook), adjust the pressure to High and the time to 3 minutes. After cooking, quick-release the pressure. Unlock and remove the lid.

3   Add the lemon juice and 150g (5oz) of the cheese to the soup. Stir until the cheese has melted, then use a hand-held blender (or a jug blender) to purée the soup. Season with black pepper and ladle into warmed bowls. Scatter the remaining cheese over the top before serving.

COOK'S NOTES

- For a really smooth soup, pass through a fine sieve. If necessary, reheat in your Instant Pot by selecting Sauté and adjusting the temperature to More for a high heat. Turn off when the soup is piping hot; do not let it boil or it may curdle.
- Any type of slightly crumbly blue cheese can be used for this soup. Stilton and Saint Agur both work well.

Chilled Avocado Soup

(v)

A chilled soup is fantastic on a hot summer day. This delicate pale green avocado version has a creamy leek base which can be made up to a day in advance in your Instant Pot.

SERVES 4

15ml (1 tbsp) avocado oil or olive oil
350g (12oz) leeks, halved lengthways and thinly sliced
600ml (1 pint) vegetable stock, preferably home-made (page 45)
Salt and white pepper
1 large ripe avocado
75ml (5 tbsp) Greek yogurt
15ml (1 tbsp) lime juice
30ml (2 tbsp) chopped fresh coriander, plus a few sprigs to garnish

1   Preheat your Instant Pot by selecting Sauté and adjust to Normal for medium heat. Add the oil and when it is hot, add the leeks. Stir well, cover with a lid and cook for 3–4 minutes, stirring frequently, until almost soft. If the mixture starts to stick, add a spoonful or two of the stock. Turn off the Sauté function.
2   Pour in the stock and season with salt and pepper. Put on the lid and lock into place. Turn the pressure-release switch to Sealing. Press Manual (Pressure Cook), adjust the pressure to High and the time to 3 minutes. After cooking, allow the pressure to release naturally for 5 minutes, then quick-release the remaining pressure. Unlock and remove the lid.

3 Leave the soup to cool slightly, then purée in your Instant Pot using a hand-held blender, or in a jug blender. Leave to cool completely, then chill well.

4 Shortly before serving, halve the avocado and discard the stone. Remove the flesh from the skin, then press it through a fine nylon or stainless-steel sieve. Stir into the soup with the yogurt, lime juice and chopped coriander. Season to taste with salt and pepper. Ladle the soup into bowls and garnish each with a sprig of fresh coriander.

Italian Vegetable Soup

SERVES 4

15ml (1 tbsp) olive oil
1 onion, chopped
1 clove garlic, crushed
1 carrot, peeled and finely diced
1 stick celery, finely diced
15ml (1 tbsp) tomato purée
750ml (1¼ pints) hot vegetable stock, preferably home-made (page 45)
1 bay leaf
400g (14oz) can butterbeans, drained and rinsed, or 200g (7oz) cooked butterbeans (page 8)
400g (14oz) can chopped tomatoes
Salt and freshly ground black pepper
75g (3oz) small pasta shapes
15ml (1 tbsp) green pesto
Freshly grated Parmesan cheese, to serve

1 Preheat your Instant Pot by selecting Sauté and adjust to Normal for medium heat. Add the oil and let it heat for a minute, then add the onion. Cook for 3–4 minutes, stirring frequently, until almost soft, then stir in the garlic, followed by the carrot, celery, tomato purée and a few spoonfuls of stock. Stir until the tomato purée has blended into the stock.

2 Pour in the rest of the stock, add the bay leaf, butterbeans, tomatoes, salt and pepper. Stir well, then scatter the pasta over the top. Cancel the Sauté function.

3 Lock the lid into place. Select Manual (Pressure Cook), adjust the pressure to High and the time to 10 minutes. After cooking, quick-release the pressure. Unlock and remove the lid.

4 Stir the pesto into the soup, ladle into warmed bowls and serve with grated Parmesan cheese.

3

Meat

Your Instant Pot is ideal for cooking all kinds of meat, but it's especially good for tougher cuts such as beef brisket and spare ribs. You can also cook leaner cuts, including braising steak and pork chops, keeping them moist and tender by marinating or braising in a gravy or sauce. Minced meats can be made into midweek meals such as bolognaise sauce and meatloaf.

Because meat doesn't brown in your Instant Pot, many recipes start by sautéing the meat. As your Instant Pot is deep and slender, chunks of meat can become overcrowded and steam rather than sear, so either cook in batches, or, as explained in recipes such as Beef in Red Wine and Steak Puff Pie, brown the meat in one piece, then cut into smaller pieces.

Beef in Beer Pot Roast

Beef brisket is often slowly braised, but can be cooked in a fraction of the time in your Instant Pot. Cooking in beer helps to make it tender and moist, as well as producing a dark, richly flavoured sauce.

SERVES 4

1–1.25kg (2¼–2¾lb) boned and rolled beef brisket joint
Salt and freshly ground black pepper
30ml (2 tbsp) sunflower oil
200ml (7fl oz) brown ale or stout
200ml (7fl oz) beef stock, preferably home-made (page 42)
1 bay leaf
1 sprig fresh rosemary
500g (1¼lb) waxy potatoes, peeled and cut into large chunks
2 carrots, peeled and cut into large chunks
2 parsnips, peeled and cut into large chunks

1   Pat the beef dry with kitchen paper and lightly season all over with salt and pepper. Preheat your Instant Pot by pressing Sauté, then adjust to More for a high heat. When it is hot, add the oil, then add the beef and sear, turning frequently, until well browned on all sides. Cancel the Sauté function.

2   Pour the ale or stout into the pot and let it bubble in the residual heat, scraping any brown bits from the bottom of the pot, then add the stock, bay leaf and rosemary.

3   Put on the lid and lock into place. Press Meat/Stew and adjust the pressure to High and the time to 40 minutes. After cooking, allow the pressure to release naturally for 10 minutes, then quick-release the remaining pressure. Unlock and remove the lid. Lift out the beef onto a warmed plate, cover with foil and leave to rest while cooking the vegetables.

4 Add the potatoes, carrots and parsnips to your Instant Pot. Put the lid back on, lock into place, select Manual (Pressure Cook), adjust the pressure to High and the time to 6 minutes. After cooking, quick-release the pressure. Unlock and remove the lid.

5 While the vegetables are cooking, cut the beef against the grain into thin slices. Serve on warmed plates with the vegetables and the gravy.

Steak Puff Pie with Mustard Gravy

You can't cook puff pastry in your Instant Pot, but this pie-making method is how restaurants produce a perfectly cooked meat filling topped with crisp pastry. Serve this with mashed potatoes and steamed fresh green vegetables.

SERVES 4

500g (1¼lb) braising steak
30ml (2 tbsp) sunflower oil
100g (4oz) baby button mushrooms
1 large onion, chopped
15ml (1 tbsp) plain flour
2.5ml (½ tsp) English mustard powder
350ml (12fl oz) hot beef stock, preferably home-made
   (page 42), or a mixture of stock and red wine
15ml (1 tbsp) Worcestershire sauce
15ml (1 tbsp) tomato purée
2 bay leaves
Salt and freshly ground black pepper
375g (13oz) pack ready-rolled puff pastry
Beaten egg, or milk, to glaze

1 Trim the meat and pat dry with kitchen paper. Preheat your Instant Pot by selecting Sauté and adjust to More for high heat. Add the oil and heat for a minute, then quickly sear the beef, turning once to brown both sides. Transfer to a board and cut into 2.5cm (1in) chunks.

2 Leaving the pot on high heat, add the mushrooms and cook, stirring occasionally, for 2–3 minutes until browned. Lift out of the pot with a slotted spoon and add to the beef. Press Keep Warm/Cancel, then press Sauté again and adjust to Less for a low heat. Add the onion and fry for 3–4 minutes until soft. If it starts to stick to the bottom of the pan, add a spoonful or two of the stock. Cancel the Sauté function.

3 Sprinkle the flour and mustard powder over the onions and stir well. Return the beef with any juices and mushrooms to the pot. Mix together the stock, Worcestershire sauce and tomato purée and pour into the pot. Add the bay leaves and season with salt and pepper. Stir well.

4 Lock the lid into place, select Meat/Stew and adjust the pressure to High and the time to 30 minutes. After cooking, allow the pressure to release naturally for 10 minutes, then quick-release the remaining pressure. Unlock and remove the lid.

5 While the beef is cooking, preheat the oven to 200°C/400°F/Gas mark 6. Unroll the pastry and, using a dinner plate as a guide, cut out a 25cm (10in) round. Transfer the pastry round to a baking sheet lined with baking parchment. Mark the pastry into quarters with a sharp knife, cutting almost, but not quite, through it. Use the pastry trimmings to add pastry leaves to the round, if liked, and crimp the edges. Lightly brush the pastry with beaten egg or milk, then bake for 15–20 minutes, or until well-risen and golden brown.

6 To serve, remove the bay leaves and spoon the beef filling mixture onto warmed serving plates. Cut the baked pie crust into four, following the markings, and top each portion of beef with a wedge of pastry. Serve straight away.

COOK'S NOTES
- You can now buy ready-rolled 'light' puff pastry with a reduced fat content.
- If the beef is ready before the pastry, allow the pressure to release naturally, press the Keep Warm button and leave in your Instant Pot until ready to serve.

Beef in Red Wine

This version of the slow-cooked Boeuf Bourguignon is ready in under an hour. It's delicious served simply with creamy mashed potatoes (page 184) and a green vegetable such as French or runner beans.

SERVES 4

12 button onions
30ml (2 tbsp) olive oil
75g (3oz) streaky bacon rashers, rind removed, diced
500g (1¼lb) lean braising steak
175g (6oz) baby mushrooms, halved
1 clove garlic, crushed
30ml (2 tbsp) plain flour
250ml (8fl oz) Burgundy or other full-bodied red wine
1 bay leaf
1 sprig fresh thyme
150ml (¼ pint) beef stock, preferably home-made (page 42)
Salt and freshly ground black pepper

1 Put the button onions in a heatproof bowl and pour over enough boiling water to cover. Leave for 5 minutes, then drain. When cool enough to handle, peel off the skins (they should slip off easily).
2 Preheat your Instant Pot by pressing Sauté and adjust to Normal for a medium heat. When hot, add 15ml (1 tbsp) of the oil and cook the bacon for 2–3 minutes until lightly browned. Remove from the pot with a slotted spoon, leaving all the fat behind, and set aside.
3 Pat the beef dry on kitchen paper. Add to the pot and briefly brown on both sides. Transfer to a board and cut into 2.5cm (1in) cubes.

4   Add the remaining 15ml (1 tbsp) oil to the pot. Add the
    onions and cook for 2 minutes, then add the mushrooms and
    garlic and cook for a further minute, stirring. Sprinkle over
    the flour and stir, then gradually add the wine. Let it come to
    the boil and bubble for a minute or two (this will allow the
    alcohol from the wine to evaporate).
5   Cancel the Sauté function and return the beef and bacon to
    the pot with the bay leaf and thyme. Pour in the stock and
    season with salt and pepper. Stir well.
6   Put on the lid and lock into place. Turn the pressure-release
    switch to Sealing. Press Meat/Stew and adjust to Normal;
    the time will automatically set to 35 minutes. After cooking,
    allow the pressure to release naturally. Remove the lid and
    serve on warmed plates.

Mushroom-stuffed Beef Rolls

Lean slices of beef are wrapped around a rich mushroom filling and cooked in a vegetable sauce with new potatoes to make a complete meal. Sometimes known as beef olives, these are perfect for entertaining and can be made in advance and kept chilled in the fridge for up to 24 hours before cooking.

SERVES 4

For the mushroom filling
15g (½oz) dried porcini mushrooms
30ml (2 tbsp) olive oil
1 onion, finely chopped
1 clove garlic, crushed
150g (5oz) chestnut mushrooms, finely chopped
25g (1oz) fresh breadcrumbs
45ml (3 tbsp) finely chopped fresh parsley
Finely grated zest of 1 lemon
Salt and freshly ground black pepper

For the beef olives
500g (1¼lb) beef topside, cut into 8 very thin slices
60ml (4 tbsp) dry sherry
1 bay leaf
350g (12oz) baby new potatoes
300ml (½ pint) beef stock, preferably home-made (page 42)

1   For the filling, put the dried porcini mushrooms in a heatproof bowl and pour over enough boiling water to cover. Leave to soak for 20 minutes. Drain and finely chop.
2   Preheat your Instant Pot by pressing Sauté and adjust to Normal for medium heat. Add 15ml (1 tbsp) of the olive oil and fry the onion for 4–5 minutes until soft. Spoon half of the onion mixture into a bowl and set aside. Add the garlic

and chopped chestnut mushrooms to your Instant Pot and cook for a further 2 minutes, stirring frequently, until soft. If the mixture starts to stick, add a spoonful of the stock. Cancel the Sauté function.

3   Remove the onion and mushroom mixture from the pot and place in a small bowl. Add the chopped porcini mushrooms, breadcrumbs, parsley and lemon zest. Season with salt and pepper and mix well.

4   Place the beef slices, one at time, between two sheets of baking parchment or cling film and gently bash out as thinly as possible using a rolling pin. Lay them side by side on a board, then divide the mushroom filling equally between them. Roll up each slice around the stuffing and secure in place with wooden cocktail sticks.

5   Heat the remaining 15ml (1 tbsp) oil in a large non-stick frying pan, add the stuffed beef rolls and fry them on a moderate heat to brown them all over.

6   Return the reserved onion mixture to your Instant Pot. Select Sauté and adjust to Normal for medium heat. Pour in the sherry and when it boils, let it bubble for about 30 seconds (to concentrate and allow the alcohol to evaporate). Turn off the Sauté function. Add the beef rolls to the pot and tuck in the bay leaf. Place the new potatoes on top, then pour over the stock.

7   Put on the lid and lock into place. Turn the pressure-release switch to Sealing. Press Manual (Pressure Cook), adjust the pressure to High and the time to 10 minutes. After cooking, allow the pressure to release naturally for 5 minutes, then quick-release the remaining pressure. Unlock and remove the lid. Transfer the beef and potatoes to warmed plates and spoon over some of the stock.

Bolognaise Sauce

This classic meat sauce served with spaghetti or pasta shapes cooks in just 15 minutes in your Instant Pot. Rather than thickening with something like cornflour, red lentils are added to the Bolognaise; they are unnoticeable in the finished dish, but give the sauce a thicker, richer consistency as well as adding protein and stretching the meat a little further.

SERVES 4

15ml (1 tbsp) olive oil
1 onion, finely chopped
450g (1lb) lean minced beef
1 clove garlic, crushed
1 medium carrot, finely chopped
1 stick celery, finely chopped
25g (1oz) red lentils, rinsed and drained
400g (14oz) can chopped tomatoes
15ml (1 tbsp) tomato purée
300ml (½ pint) hot beef stock, preferably home-made
   (page 42)
150ml (¼ pint) red wine or extra 150ml (¼ pint) beef stock
2.5ml (½ tsp) dried oregano or mixed herbs
1 bay leaf
Salt and freshly ground black pepper
30ml (2 tbsp) chopped fresh parsley (optional)
Cooked spaghetti or pasta shapes and grated Parmesan
   cheese, to serve

1   Preheat your Instant Pot by selecting Sauté and adjust to Normal for medium heat. Add the oil and wait until hot, then add the onion and cook for 3 minutes, stirring frequently, until it begins to soften.

2   Still using the Sauté function, adjust the heat to More for a high heat. Add the beef and cook, stirring, until browned, breaking up the lumps of meat with a wooden spoon. Add the garlic, carrot and celery and stir for a further 2 minutes.

3   Stir in the lentils, followed by the chopped tomatoes. Combine the tomato purée with the beef stock and add to your Instant Pot with the wine or extra stock, oregano and bay leaf, salt and pepper. Cancel the Sauté setting.

4   Put on the lid and lock into place. Select Manual (Pressure Cook) and adjust the pressure to High and the time to 10 minutes. After cooking, allow the pressure to release naturally for 10 minutes, then quick-release the remaining pressure. Unlock and remove the lid.

5   Taste and adjust the seasoning if necessary and stir in the fresh parsley, if using. Ladle over bowls of freshly cooked pasta and sprinkle with grated Parmesan before serving.

Chilli Con Carne

Tiny chunks of beef are cooked with beans and spiced with chillies and cumin. This is a warming meal, ideal for casual entertaining, served with hot crusty bread or cornbread (page 226).

SERVES 4

30ml (2 tbsp) olive oil
350g (12oz) lean braising steak, trimmed and cut into 1cm (½in) cubes
1 large onion, chopped
2 cloves garlic, crushed
5ml (1 tsp) ground cumin
5ml (1 tsp) cacao or cocoa powder
2.5ml (½ tsp) crushed dried red chillies
15ml (1 tbsp) tomato purée
400g (14oz) can chopped tomatoes
400g (14oz) can red kidney beans, drained and rinsed, or 250g (9oz) cooked red kidney beans (page 8)
300ml (½ pint) beef stock, preferably home-made (page 42)
Salt and freshly ground black pepper
Sour cream and green salad, to serve

1   Preheat your Instant Pot by selecting Sauté and adjust to More for a high heat. Add 15ml (1 tbsp) of oil, let it heat for a few seconds, then add the beef. Fry for 3–4 minutes, stirring occasionally, until well browned. Remove the meat with a slotted spoon and set aside.

2 Cancel, then select Sauté again, this time adjusting to Less for a low heat. Add the remaining oil and the onion and cook gently for 5–6 minutes, stirring frequently, until starting to brown. Add the garlic and cook for a few seconds, then add the cumin, cacao or cocoa and the chillies. Stir in the tomato purée, chopped tomatoes, beans and stock. Return the beef to the pot and season with salt and pepper.

3 Put on the lid, lock into place and turn the pressure-release switch to Sealing. Press the Manual (Pressure Cook) button, adjust the pressure to High and the time to 15 minutes.

4 When cooking is complete, allow the pressure to release naturally for 10 minutes, then quick-release the remaining pressure. Unlock and remove the lid. Serve in warmed bowls, topped with a spoonful of sour cream and accompanied with a green salad and warm crusty bread or cornbread.

Beef Massaman Curry

The potatoes in this rich Thai curry soak up all the flavour of the sauce and help to thicken the dish. It makes a meal on its own, or you can serve it with jasmine rice, if you like.

SERVES 4

400ml (14fl oz) can coconut milk
45ml (3 tbsp) massaman curry paste
450g (1lb) braising steak, cut into 2.5cm (1in) pieces
15ml (1 tbsp) tamarind paste
100ml (4fl oz) beef stock, preferably home-made (page 42)
1 onion, very thinly sliced
½ cinnamon stick
3 kaffir lime leaves
15ml (1 tbsp) light soft brown sugar
15ml (1 tbsp) Thai fish sauce
450g (1lb) waxy potatoes, cut into 2.5cm (1in) chunks
75g (3oz) unsalted toasted peanuts, roughly chopped
Salt and freshly ground black pepper

1   Preheat your Instant Pot by selecting Sauté and adjust to More for high heat. Add 60ml (4 tbsp) coconut milk and the curry paste. Stir together, then heat until bubbling. Add the beef and fry for 3–4 minutes until coated in the spice mixture.

2   Stir in the tamarind paste, then add the remaining coconut milk, stock, onion, cinnamon stick, lime leaves, sugar and fish sauce and stir well. Cancel the Sauté function.

3 Put on the lid and lock into place. Select Meat/Stew and adjust the pressure to High. The time should automatically set to 35 minutes. After cooking, quick-release the pressure and remove the lid. Stir in the potatoes and two-thirds of the peanuts. Put the lid back on, select Manual (Pressure Cook) and adjust the time to 5 minutes.

4 After cooking, naturally release the pressure for 5 minutes, then quick-release any remaining pressure. Unlock and remove the lid. Stir, then season the curry to taste with salt and pepper. Spoon onto warmed plates and serve scattered with the remaining chopped peanuts.

Italian Meatballs in Rich Tomato Sauce

In these tender little meatballs, fresh breadcrumbs soak up all the flavours and make the meat go further. The tasty tomato sauce already contains vegetables, so all you need to complete the meal is some quickly cooked tagliatelle.

SERVES 4

350g (12oz) lean minced beef
50g (2oz) fresh white breadcrumbs
2 cloves garlic, crushed
60ml (4 tbsp) freshly grated Parmesan cheese
5ml (1 tsp) dried mixed herbs
1 medium egg yolk
Salt and freshly ground black pepper
15ml (1 tbsp) olive oil
1 large onion, finely chopped
400g (14oz) can chopped tomatoes
1 large carrot, peeled and grated
100ml (4fl oz) red wine, or vegetable stock, preferably home-made (page 45)
30ml (2 tbsp) shredded fresh basil, or chopped fresh parsley

1 Put the beef, breadcrumbs, 1 crushed clove garlic, 15ml (1 tbsp) of the Parmesan, the mixed herbs and egg yolk in a bowl. Season well with salt and pepper. Work together with your hands until evenly mixed. With dampened hands to stop the mixture sticking, shape into 12 even-sized balls.

2 Preheat your Instant Pot by selecting Sauté and adjust to Normal for medium heat. When it is hot, add the oil, then add the onion and cook for 3–4 minutes, stirring frequently, until softened. Add the remaining crushed clove of garlic and cook for a few more seconds.

3 Cancel the Sauté function and add the chopped tomatoes, carrot and red wine or stock. Season with salt and pepper and stir well. Add the meatballs to the sauce.

4 Put on the lid and lock into place. Turn the pressure-release switch to Sealing. Press Manual (Pressure Cook), adjust the pressure to High and the time to 5 minutes. After cooking, allow the pressure to release naturally for 10 minutes, then quick-release the remaining pressure. Unlock and remove the lid.

5 Spoon the meatballs into a warmed bowl. Stir the basil or parsley into the tomato sauce. Spoon the sauce over cooked pasta and top with the meatballs. Sprinkle the remaining Parmesan on top.

Easy Meatloaf with New Potatoes and Carrots

Cooking a complete meal in your Instant Pot is easy – simply use your steaming rack (trivet) to separate the meatloaf from the vegetables. A round tin is preferable to a square or loaf-shaped tin as it will ensure even cooking.

SERVES 4

For the meatloaf
15ml (1 tbsp) sunflower oil
1 onion, finely chopped
1 clove garlic, crushed
1 stick celery, finely chopped
225g (8oz) minced beef
225g (8oz) minced pork
25g (1oz) porridge oats
5ml (1 tsp) dried mixed herbs
1 medium egg
5ml (1 tsp) Dijon mustard
Salt and freshly ground black pepper

For the vegetables
675g (1½lb) new potatoes, halved if large
300g (11oz) baby carrots, trimmed
250ml (8fl oz) vegetable or beef stock, preferably home-made (see pages 42 and 45)

1   Line the base of a 16cm (6½in) fixed-base round tin, at least 5cm (2in) deep, with baking parchment. Preheat your Instant Pot by selecting the Sauté function. When the inner cooking pot is hot, add the oil, then add the onion and cook for 3–4 minutes, stirring frequently. Add the garlic and celery and cook for a further 2 minutes. Cancel the Sauté function.

2   Tip and scrape the onion mixture into a bowl. Allow to cool for
    a few minutes, then add the beef, pork, oats and dried herbs.
    Beat the egg together with the mustard. Add to the mixture
    and season well with salt and pepper. Mix everything together
    with your hands and gently press into the tin, levelling the top
    fairly smooth. Cover with a piece of foil.

3   Put the new potatoes and carrots into the inner pot (there's no
    need to wash it out first) and put the steaming rack (trivet) on
    top. Pour in the stock. Place the meatloaf on top of the trivet.

4   Close the lid and lock into place. Turn the pressure-release
    switch to Sealing. Press Manual (Pressure Cook), adjust the
    pressure to High and the time to 15 minutes. After cooking,
    allow the pressure to release naturally for 5 minutes, then quick-
    release the remaining pressure. Unlock and remove the lid.

5   Lift out the meatloaf and place on a wire rack to let it settle
    for a few minutes. Spoon the vegetables onto warmed plates.
    Run a blunt knife around the edge of the tin, turn out the
    meatloaf and remove the lining paper. Cut into four wedges
    and serve straight away.

COOK'S NOTE
- If liked, the top of the meatloaf can be browned by placing
  under a hot grill for a few minutes.

VARIATION
- For Chilli Bean Meatloaf, substitute ½ green pepper, seeded and
  finely chopped, for the celery and add a 200g (7oz) can red
  kidney beans, drained and rinsed, or 125g (4½oz) cooked red
  kidney beans (page 8), instead of the oats. Add 5ml (1 tsp) hot
  chilli powder and 2.5ml (½ tsp) ground paprika to the mixture.

Mongolian Beef

This is a classic quick-cook beef dish using already-tender beefsteak. Ideally, let the meat marinate for several hours in the fridge and use a non-stick inner pot, if you have one.

SERVES 4

400g (14oz) rump steak, trimmed

For the marinade
10ml (2 tsp) sesame oil
10ml (2 tsp) rice or sherry vinegar

For the sauce
1 carrot, peeled
25ml (5 tsp) sunflower or groundnut oil
1 clove garlic, crushed
15ml (1 tbsp) finely grated fresh ginger
4 spring onions, trimmed and cut into 2cm (¾in) lengths
15ml (1 tbsp) rice wine or sherry
2.5ml (½ tsp) Chinese five-spice powder
Pinch of dried red chillies or chilli powder
45ml (3 tbsp) hoisin sauce
5ml (1 tsp) soft dark brown sugar
75ml (5 tbsp) vegetable stock, preferably home-made (page 00), or water

1 Slice the beef thinly, then cut into 1cm (½in) wide strips. Mix together the sesame oil and rice or sherry vinegar in a bowl. Add the beef and toss together to coat. Cover with cling film and leave to marinate in the fridge for at least 1 hour and up to 12 hours.
2 When ready to cook, cut the carrot into 5cm (2in) lengths, then cut into matchstick strips. Pat the beef dry on kitchen paper.

3 Preheat your Instant Pot by selecting Sauté and adjust to More for a high heat. When the pot is hot, add 10ml (2 tsp) of the sunflower or groundnut oil. Add half of the beef and fry for about 30 seconds, stirring all the time; it should be browned in places, but not cooked. Remove from the pot and transfer to a plate. Repeat with 10ml (2 tsp) more oil and the remaining beef. Cancel the Sauté function.

4 Add the remaining 5ml (1 tsp) of oil to the pot; it should still be really hot. Add the garlic and ginger and cook for about 30 seconds, then add the carrots and spring onions. Stir for a minute, then pour in the rice wine or sherry.

5 Add the five-spice powder, dried chillies, hoisin sauce and sugar. Stir, then pour in the vegetable stock or water. Return the beef and any juices to your Instant Pot and mix well.

6 Put on the lid and lock into place. Turn the pressure-release switch to Sealing. Press Manual (Pressure Cook), adjust the pressure to High and the time to 2 minutes. After cooking, allow the pressure to release naturally for 5 minutes, then quick-release the remaining pressure.

7 Unlock and remove the lid. Stir the beef and serve on warmed plates on top of jasmine rice or fine noodles.

Venison and Beetroot Casserole

Venison is full-flavoured but lower in fat than beef. Here, it is slow-cooked with fresh beetroot and chestnuts to ensure the meat is wonderfully tender and has absorbed all the flavours.

SERVES 4

15ml (1 tbsp) olive oil
450g (1lb) boneless venison haunch or shoulder, cut into
    4cm (1½in) cubes
15g (½oz) unsalted butter
1 large onion, sliced
1 clove garlic, crushed
2.5cm (1in) piece fresh ginger, peeled and grated
75ml (5 tbsp) port (use red wine if you don't have port)
2 raw beetroot, about 150g (5oz) each, peeled and cut into
    8 wedges
Pared strip of orange zest
300ml (½ pint) beef stock, preferably home-made (page 42)
100g (4oz) vacuum-packed peeled whole chestnuts
Salt and freshly ground black pepper

1   Preheat your Instant Pot by selecting Sauté and adjust to
    Normal for medium heat. Add the olive oil and when hot, add
    the venison. Cook, stirring frequently, for 3–4 minutes, until
    browned on all sides. Remove from the pot and set aside.
2   Add the butter to the pot and when melted add the onion.
    Cook for 3–4 minutes until beginning to soften, then add the
    garlic and ginger and cook for a few seconds. Pour in the port
    and let it bubble, then cancel the Sauté function.

3 Return the venison to the pot with the beetroot, orange zest, stock and chestnuts. Season with salt and pepper and stir well.

4 Put on the lid and lock into place. Turn the pressure-release switch to Venting. Press Slow Cook and adjust to More for a high heat; the time should automatically set to 4 hours. After cooking, unlock and remove the lid and serve the casserole on warmed plates with Creamy Mashed Potatoes (page 184).

Tuscan-style Shoulder of Lamb

With all the benefits of fast pressure-cooking, it's easy to forget that your Instant Pot can be used as a slow cooker too. This rolled shoulder of lamb is slow cooked until meltingly tender in typical Tuscan recipe, in which simple flavours are combined with good-quality ingredients.

SERVES 4

15ml (1 tbsp) olive oil
1.2–1.3kg (2½–3lb) lamb shoulder, trimmed, boned and tied
3 cloves garlic, peeled and cut into quarters, lengthways
12 small sprigs fresh rosemary
1 onion, chopped
3 carrots, finely chopped
1 leek, halved lengthways and thinly sliced
150ml (¼ pint) red wine
300ml (½ pint) vegetable stock, preferably home-made
  (page 45)
400g (14oz) can chopped tomatoes
2 bay leaves
400g (14oz) can cannellini beans, drained and rinsed, or
  225g (8oz) cooked cannellini beans (page 8)
Salt and freshly ground black pepper
Washed or new potatoes and green beans, to serve

1 Heat the oil in a large non-stick frying pan and brown the
   lamb on all sides. Remove from the pan and when cool
   enough to handle, make 12 deep incisions, evenly spaced,
   over the top and sides of the lamb and insert a sliver of garlic
   and sprig of rosemary into each.

2   Tip any excess fat out of the pan, leaving about 15ml (1 tbsp) behind, then add the onion and cook for 3–4 minutes until lightly coloured. Add the carrots and leek and cook for a few more minutes until beginning to soften, then transfer to your inner pot.

3   Pour the wine into the frying pan and let it bubble for a minute, stirring to dissolve any crusty bits on the bottom of the pan. Pour over the vegetables in your Instant Pot. Add the stock, tomatoes and bay leaves to the pot. Season with a little salt and pepper and stir well. Place the lamb on top.

4   Put on the lid and lock into place. Turn the pressure-release switch to Venting. Press Slow Cook and adjust to Normal for a medium heat; the time should automatically set to 4 hours.

5   After cooking, unlock and remove the lid and lift out the lamb. Put on a warmed plate, cover with foil to keep warm and leave to rest for 10 minutes.

6   Press Sauté and adjust to Normal for a medium heat. Skim any fat from the top of the vegetable mixture, then stir in the cannellini beans. Let the mixture bubble for 10 minutes to reduce the juices.

7   Remove the string from the lamb and carve. Discard the bay leaves and spoon the vegetables and beans onto warmed plates. Arrange the lamb slices on top. Serve with mashed or new potatoes and steamed green beans.

COOK'S NOTE
- Cannellini beans are traditionally served with this dish, but you can use butter beans or flageolet beans if you prefer.

Braised Lamb Shanks with Borlotti Beans

Lamb shanks are best cooked with the slow cook setting of your Instant Pot. Full of flavour, each shank makes a perfect individual portion. Balsamic vinegar is dark and mellow and adds a richness and depth to the sauce.

SERVES 4

4 lamb shanks
30ml (2 tbsp) olive oil
1 onion, chopped
2 carrots, peeled and diced
2 sticks celery, thinly sliced
1 clove garlic, crushed
30ml (2 tbsp) balsamic vinegar
300ml (½ pint) vegetable stock, preferably home-made (page 45)
400g (14oz) can chopped tomatoes
5ml (1 tsp) dried Mediterranean herbs or oregano
1 sprig fresh rosemary
1 bay leaf
Salt and freshly ground black pepper
400g (14oz) can borlotti beans, drained or 250g (9oz) cooked borlotti beans (page 8)

1   Remove any excess fat from the lamb shanks and pat dry on kitchen paper. Preheat your Instant Pot by selecting Sauté and adjust to More for a high heat. Add the oil and when it is hot, add the lamb shanks and brown on all sides. Lift out onto a plate, leaving the fat behind in the pot.

2 Select Sauté again and adjust to Normal for a medium heat. Add the onion and cook for 3–4 minutes, stirring frequently. Add the carrots, celery and garlic and cook for 2 more minutes. Stir in the vinegar, then cancel the Sauté function.

3 Stir in the stock, chopped tomatoes and dried herbs. Add the rosemary and bay leaf and season with salt and pepper. Return the lamb shanks to the pot together with any juices on the plate.

4 Put on the lid and lock into place. Turn the pressure-release switch to Venting. Press Slow Cook and adjust to Normal for a medium heat; the time should automatically set to 4 hours.

5 After cooking, unlock and remove the lid and lift out the lamb shanks. Put on a warmed plate, cover with foil to keep warm and leave to rest for 5 minutes.

6 Press Sauté and adjust to More for a high heat. Skim any fat from the top of the vegetable mixture, then stir in the beans. Let the mixture bubble for 5 minutes to reduce the juices a little. Serve the lamb on warm plates and spoon over the bean and vegetable sauce.

COOK'S NOTE
- If the lamb shanks are large, you may have to brown them two at a time. Alternatively, brown them in a large non-stick frying pan.

Lamb Stifado

Stifado is a meaty Greek stew with a rich herby sauce. If possible, use a tin of peeled cherry tomatoes rather than plum tomatoes as they have a sweeter flavour. A sprinkling of feta cheese adds a finishing flourish to the dish. Warm crusty bread makes a great accompaniment.

SERVES 4

12 shallots
30ml (2 tbsp) olive oil
675g (1½lb) lean lamb neck fillet, trimmed of fat and sliced
2 cloves garlic, crushed
30ml (2 tbsp) red wine vinegar
2.5ml (½ tsp) caster sugar
150ml (¼ pint) red wine
150ml (¼ pint) vegetable stock, preferably home-made (page 45)
400g (14oz) can peeled cherry tomatoes or chopped tomatoes
10ml (2 tsp) chopped fresh oregano
1 bay leaf
1 cinnamon stick
Salt and freshly ground black pepper
100g (4oz) feta cheese, crumbled, to serve

1 Put the shallots in a heatproof bowl. Pour over enough boiling water to cover and leave for 5 minutes. Drain and when cool enough to handle, peel off the skins (they should slip off easily).

2 Preheat your Instant Pot by selecting Sauté and adjust to Normal for medium heat. Add 15ml (1 tbsp) of the oil and when hot, add the lamb and fry for 3–4 minutes, until browned all over. Remove from the pot and set aside.

3 Add the remaining 15ml (1 tbsp) of oil to the pot. Add the shallots and fry for 2–3 minutes, stirring frequently, until lightly browned. Add the garlic, vinegar, sugar and wine. Bring to the boil and let the mixture bubble for about 30 seconds (to allow the alcohol to evaporate). Cancel the Sauté function.

4 Return the meat to the pot and add the stock, tomatoes, oregano, bay leaf and cinnamon stick. Season with salt (very lightly, as the feta contains plenty) and pepper. Stir well.

5 Put on the lid and lock into place. Turn the pressure-release switch to Sealing. Press Manual (Pressure Cook), adjust the pressure to High and the time to 25 minutes. After cooking, allow the pressure to release naturally for 10 minutes, then quick-release the remaining pressure. Serve on warmed plates with the feta crumbled over.

Lamb Rogan Josh

This renowned Kashmiri dish is marinated overnight in the fridge, creating melt-in-the mouth meat in a rich spiced sauce. It's healthier than any ready-meal or takeaway.

SERVES 4

7.5ml (1½ tsp) garam masala
5ml (1 tsp) smoked paprika
5ml (1 tsp) salt
2.5ml (½ tsp) ground turmeric
2.5ml (½ tsp) ground cinnamon
1.5ml (¼ tsp) freshly grated nutmeg
1.5ml (¼ tsp) cayenne pepper
2 cloves garlic, crushed
30ml (2 tbsp) tomato purée
90ml (6 tbsp) Greek yogurt (page 30)
60ml (4 tbsp) cold water
1 onion, finely chopped
450g (1lb) boneless lamb, e.g. leg, cut into 2.5cm (1in) cubes

1 Put the garam masala, paprika, salt, turmeric, cinnamon, nutmeg, cayenne pepper, garlic and tomato paste in a glass bowl (or you can use your stainless-steel inner pot if you prefer). Stir in the Greek yogurt a spoonful at a time, blending everything together. Stir in the water.
2 Add the onion and lamb and mix well, coating the meat in the spicy mixture. Tightly cover with cling film and allow to marinate in the fridge for at least 4 hours, preferably overnight and up to 24 hours.

3 Transfer the mixture to your Instant Pot. Put on the lid and lock into place. Turn the pressure-release switch to Sealing. Press Manual (Pressure Cook), adjust the pressure to High and the time to 20 minutes.

4 When cooking is complete, allow the pressure to release naturally. Unlock and remove the lid, give the curry a stir and serve on warmed plates.

COOK'S NOTE
- Use full-fat Greek yogurt for this dish, as low fat and Greek-style yogurts will separate during cooking, resulting in a curdled sauce.

Normandy Pork with Apples and Walnuts

Pork and apples are perfect partners. This casserole originates from northwestern France, where apple orchards are abundant and many gardens have their own walnut trees.

SERVES 4

100g (4oz) broken walnuts
30ml (2 tbsp) sunflower oil
400g (14oz) pork fillet, trimmed of fat and cut into 2cm (¾in) cubes
1 onion, chopped
1 clove garlic, crushed
2 sticks celery, thickly sliced
200ml (7fl oz) apple juice
150ml (¼ pint) vegetable stock, preferably home-made (page 45)
2 eating apples, preferably red-skinned, quartered, cored and thickly sliced
Salt and freshly ground black pepper
30ml (2 tbsp) crème fraiche

1   Preheat your Instant Pot by selecting Sauté and adjust to Less for a low heat. Add the walnuts and cook for 3–4 minutes, stirring frequently until they smell toasted. Remove from the pot and set aside.
2   Cancel Sauté, then press Sauté again and adjust to More for a high heat. Add the oil and when it is hot, add the pork and cook for 2–3 minutes or until lightly browned. Remove from the pot using a slotted spoon, leaving the fat behind, and set aside on a plate.

3 Add the onion to the pot and cook for 3 minutes, stirring frequently. Add the garlic and celery and cook for a further 2–3 minutes, adding a spoonful or two of apple juice if the mixture starts to stick.

4 Return the meat to the pot and add the apple juice, vegetable stock and apples. Season with salt and pepper and stir well.

5 Put on the lid and lock into place. Turn the pressure-release switch to Sealing. Press Manual (Pressure Cook), adjust the pressure to High and the time to 20 minutes. When cooking is complete, allow the pressure to release naturally. Unlock and remove the lid.

6 Blend a little of the hot juices with the crème fraiche in a small bowl, then stir into the casserole. Serve straight away, with potatoes and a green vegetable such as French beans.

Bangers and Cheesy Mash

You don't need to choose whether to use your Instant Pot for sausages or mashed potatoes: they can both be cooked at the same time.

SERVES 4

15ml (1 tbsp) sunflower oil
8 good-quality pork sausages
1 red onion, halved and thinly sliced
15g (½oz) unsalted butter
900g (2lb) potatoes, peeled and cut into 5cm (2in) chunks
250ml (8fl oz) milk
2.5ml (½ tsp) salt
Freshly ground black pepper
50g (2oz) mature Cheddar, grated

1 Preheat your non-stick inner pot by selecting Sauté and adjust to Normal for a medium heat. When hot, add the oil, then add the sausages and onion. Cook for 3–4 minutes, turning frequently, until the sausages are browned in places. Remove from the pot and transfer to a piece of foil. Wipe the pot clean with kitchen paper.
2 Cut the butter into small pieces and put in the base of your Instant Pot. Add the potatoes and sprinkle with salt and a few grinds of pepper, then pour over the milk.
3 Carefully place the foil containing the sausages and onions on top of the potatoes, crimping the edges slightly to make a bowl shape, so that there's no risk of the sausages rolling off.

4 Put on the lid and lock into place. Select Manual (Pressure Cook), adjust the pressure to High and the time to 8 minutes. After cooking, allow the pressure to release naturally for 5 minutes, then quick-release any remaining pressure. Unlock and remove the lid.

5 Lift out the sausages and onions. Mash the potatoes into the milk mixture using a potato masher, then beat with a wooden spoon until smooth and creamy. Add the grated cheese and beat again.

6 Pile the mash onto warmed plates and serve with the sausages and onions. Accompany with a green vegetable such as peas or with baked beans.

Sausage Casserole with Cider

Here meaty pork sausages are simmered in a cider sauce, which gives them a lovely subtle apple taste. If you don't have any cider, a fruity white wine can be used instead or well-flavoured vegetable stock.

SERVES 4

15ml (1 tbsp) sunflower oil
400g (14oz) high-meat-content pork sausages
2 onions, halved and thinly sliced
5ml (1 tsp) smoked paprika
5ml (1 tsp) dark muscovado sugar
5ml (1 tsp) dried mixed herbs
400g (14oz) can chopped tomatoes
150ml (¼ pint) fruity cider
150ml (¼ pint) chicken or vegetable stock, preferably home-made (pages 44–45)
2 bay leaves
Salt and freshly ground black pepper
400g (14oz) can butterbeans, drained, or 250g (9oz) cooked butterbeans (page 8)

1 Preheat your Instant Pot by selecting Sauté and adjust to Normal for medium heat. Add the oil and heat for a minute, then add the sausages, turning until browned all over. (You may find it easier to do this in a large non-stick frying pan). Lift out of the pot using a slotted spoon, leaving the oil behind, and place on a plate.

2   Leaving the pot on medium heat, add the onions and cook, stirring occasionally, for 3–4 minutes. Stir in the paprika, sugar, herbs, tomatoes, cider, stock and bay leaves. Season with salt and pepper. Return the sausages to the pot and cancel the Sauté function.

3   Put on the lid and lock into place. Turn the pressure-release switch to Sealing. Select Meat/Stew and adjust the pressure to High and the time to 10 minutes.

4   When cooking is complete, quick-release the pressure. Put the butterbeans in a sieve and rinse with boiling water. Remove the lid, add the butterbeans to the casserole and stir. Leave them for a minute or two to warm through. Serve straight away.

Oriental Pork and Cabbage Parcels

Minced pork is nowhere near as popular as minced beef, but just as tasty and versatile. Here it is used as a stuffing together with crunchy water chestnuts, fresh ginger and Chinese five-spice powder and packed into green cabbage leaves.

SERVES 4

400g (14oz) lean minced pork
225g (8oz) can water chestnuts, drained and finely chopped
4 spring onions, trimmed and finely chopped
15ml (1 tbsp) grated fresh ginger
45ml (3 tbsp) dark soy sauce
5ml (1 tsp) sesame oil
5ml (1 tsp) Chinese five-spice powder
1 medium egg, beaten
8 large green cabbage leaves, well washed
250ml (8fl oz) vegetable or chicken stock, preferably home-made (pages 44–45)
10ml (2 tsp) cornflour

1   Put the pork, water chestnuts, spring onions, ginger, 30ml (2 tbsp) of the soy sauce, the sesame oil, five-spice powder and egg in a bowl. Mix everything together, then divide the mixture into 8 equal portions.
2   Pour the stock into your inner pot and add your trivet (steaming rack). Cut off the tough stalk from the base of each cabbage leaf. Place a portion of the pork in the middle of the leaf, then wrap the leaf around the filling to enclose it. Place the parcel, seam-side down, on the trivet.

3 Repeat with the remaining cabbage leaves and pork mixture. You will need to pile up the parcels in two layers; try to leave small gaps between the parcels to allow the steam to circulate.

4 Put on the lid and lock into place. Turn the pressure-release switch to Sealing. Press Steam, adjust the pressure to High and the time to 12 minutes. After cooking, allow the pressure to release naturally for 5 minutes, then quick-release the remaining pressure.

5 Check the cabbage rolls are cooked by pressing gently on one; it should be firm. If necessary, steam for a further 3–4 minutes. Carefully remove the cabbage parcels and the trivet from your Instant Pot, then put the parcels on a warmed plate and cover with foil.

6 Blend the cornflour with the reserved 15ml (1 tbsp) soy sauce and stir into the stock. Press Sauté and adjust to Normal for a medium heat. Stir the sauce until it thickens and bubbles. Serve two cabbage parcels per person, spooning a little of the hot sauce over each. Rice (page 7) makes an excellent accompaniment.

Cider-glazed Gammon

A cold glazed gammon makes a superb centrepiece for a buffet on any occasion and can be prepared a day or two in advance. You can, of course, serve the gammon freshly cooked and hot if you prefer. Here the gammon is glazed and browned in a conventional oven towards the end of cooking. If you don't want to finish it this way, cook for an extra 30 minutes on the Slow Cook setting on your Instant Pot.

SERVES 8

2kg (4½lb) gammon joint
1 small onion, peeled
About 25 whole cloves
2 bay leaves
6 black peppercorns
150ml (¼ pint) medium or sweet cider
45ml (3 tbsp) soft light brown sugar

1   If the gammon joint is smoked, put in your inner pot, pour over enough cold water to cover and soak for at least 4 hours or overnight, in the fridge. The following day, tip away the water.
2   Place the gammon in your Instant Pot. Stud the onion with 4 of the cloves and add to the pot with the bay leaves and peppercorns. Pour over enough cold water to just cover the gammon. Cover with a pan lid , press Sauté and adjust to More for a high heat. When the water starts to boil, cancel the Sauté function and skim off the scum from the surface.
3   Remove the pan lid. Put on your Instant Pot lid and lock into place. Turn the pressure-release switch to Venting. Press Slow Cook and adjust to Normal for a medium heat; the time should automatically set to 4 hours.

4 When slow cooking is complete, unlock and remove the lid. Carefully lift the joint out of your Instant Pot and place it in a roasting tin lined with foil. Leave it to stand for about 20 minutes, or until cool enough to handle.

5 Meanwhile, discard the cooking liquid and wash the inner pot. Pour in the cider and add the sugar. Press Sauté and adjust to Normal for a medium heat. Stir as the cider heats, to dissolve the sugar, then let it bubble until reduced by about half to a sticky glaze. Cancel the Sauté function.

6 Preheat the oven to 200°C/400°F/Gas mark 6. Remove the string from the gammon, then carefully slice off the rind, leaving a thin even layer of fat over the meat. Score the fat into a neat diamond pattern and press a whole clove into the middle of each diamond. Spoon over the glaze and spread it evenly over the fat and over the two ends of the joint. Bake for 20 minutes or until the fat is a dark golden-brown. Brush with more glaze halfway through cooking.

7 Remove from the oven, cover loosely with foil and leave to rest for 15 minutes if serving hot. Alternatively, cool completely and store in the fridge until ready to serve.

COOK'S NOTE
- You can add other flavouring ingredients to the cooking water if you like, such as a strip or two of orange peel or some thinly sliced fresh ginger.

Gammon Steaks with Quick Cumberland Sauce

This is a really simple way to cook gammon. Cooking in your Instant Pot ensures that the sauce also acts as a marinade, tenderising the meat and flavouring it at the same time.

SERVES 4

Finely grated zest of 1 small lemon
Finely grated zest of 1 small orange
30ml (2 tbsp) redcurrant jelly
10ml (2 tsp) wholegrain mustard
100ml (4fl oz) red wine
100ml (4fl oz) orange juice
Freshly ground black pepper
2 smoked gammon steaks, about 225g (8oz) each,
    trimmed of fat
10ml (2 tsp) cornflour

1   Put the lemon and orange zest, redcurrant jelly, mustard and wine in your Instant Pot. Reserve 15ml (1 tbsp) of the orange juice and pour the rest into the pot. Season with a little black pepper. Press Sauté and adjust to Less for a low heat. Bring the mixture to the boil, stirring occasionally, and let it bubble for a minute to allow the alcohol to evaporate. Cancel the Sauté function.
2   Meanwhile, halve the gammon steaks and snip through the edges at 1cm (½in) intervals so that the steaks will not curl during cooking. Pat them dry with kitchen paper.

3 Pour most of the sauce out of the inner pot into a jug, leaving about 30ml (2 tbsp) behind. Add two of the gammon steak pieces, pour over some of the sauce, then top with the remaining two pieces; put them at right angles to the first two, rather than directly on top. Pour over the rest of the sauce.

4 Put on the lid, lock into place and turn the pressure-release switch to Sealing. Press Manual (Pressure Cook), adjust the pressure to Low and the time to 1 minute. After cooking, allow the pressure to release naturally for 7 minutes, then quick-release the remaining pressure. Unlock and remove the lid.

5 Lift the meat out of the sauce and put on warmed plates. Blend the cornflour with the reserved orange juice and stir into the sauce. The sauce should still be bubbling and will thicken without needing to reheat. Pour the sauce over the gammon steaks and serve straight away.

VARIATION
- For Pineapple and Mango Gammon Steaks, drain a 227g (8oz) can of pineapple rings in natural juice, reserving the juice. Cut the pineapple rings in half. Reserve 15ml (1 tbsp) pineapple juice and stir 45ml (3 tbsp) mango chutney into the rest (cut up any large pieces of mango). Prepare the gammon as the main recipe and place in your Instant Pot, with the pineapple rings sandwiched between the layers of gammon. Pour over the pineapple juice sauce. Cook as step 4, blending the cornflour with the reserved pineapple juice in step 5.

Sticky Spare Ribs

Cooking ribs in your Instant Pot will make them fall-off-the-bone tender. This is an excellent way of using up a bottle of cola that has gone flat. Alternatively, buy inexpensive 'value' cola. Make sure you choose short meaty ribs that will easily fit in your Instant Pot. The ribs are finished with the sticky glaze under a hot grill – or on the barbecue.

SERVES 4

12 meaty pork spare ribs, about 900g (2lb) in total
600ml (1 pint) cola (not sugar-free)
60ml (4 tbsp) tomato ketchup
30ml (2 tbsp) soft dark brown sugar
30ml (2 tbsp) sweet chilli sauce
15 ml (1 tbsp) dark soy sauce
15 ml (1 tbsp) Worcestershire sauce
15ml (1 tbsp) French mustard

1 Trim the spare ribs if necessary, removing excess fat, and put them in your Instant Pot, packing them as tightly as possible. Pour over the cola and let any bubbles subside (gently shake the pot a few times or give the cola a stir to speed this up), then pour in just enough water to cover the ribs; it should come no more than halfway up the pot.

2 Put on the lid and lock into place. Turn the pressure-release switch to Sealing. Press Manual (Pressure Cook), adjust the pressure to High and the time to 20 minutes. After cooking, allow the pressure to release naturally. Unlock and remove the lid. Carefully remove the ribs with tongs and when cool enough to handle, pat dry on kitchen paper.

3   Preheat the grill to high and line a grill pan with foil. Mix together the ketchup, sugar, chilli sauce, soy sauce, Worcestershire sauce and mustard. Thickly brush all over the ribs, one at a time, and place them in the grill pan.

4   Grill the ribs for a few minutes, turning frequently and brushing with more of the glaze, until dark and sticky. Serve hot with plenty of paper napkins to hold them.

VARIATION
- For Chinese Spare Ribs, make the glaze with 15ml (1 tbsp) grated fresh ginger, 45ml (3 tbsp) thick honey, 30ml (2 tbsp) dark soy sauce, 30ml (2 tbsp) rice wine or sherry, 30ml (2 tbsp) hoisin sauce and 10ml (2 tsp) sherry or balsamic vinegar.

Pork Chops in Barbecue Sauce

A sweet and sour barbecue sauce works well with rich meats such as pork and helps to tenderise the meat as it cooks.

SERVES 4

4 thick-cut boneless pork loin chops, about 150g (5oz) each, trimmed of fat
15ml (1 tbsp) sunflower oil
60ml (4 tbsp) orange juice
30ml (2 tbsp) clear honey
30ml (2 tbsp) soy sauce
30ml (2 tbsp) dry sherry
30ml (2 tbsp) balsamic vinegar
15ml (1 tbsp) Dijon mustard
15ml (1 tbsp) tomato purée
Freshly ground black pepper

1   Pat the chops dry on kitchen paper. Heat the oil in a large non-stick frying pan and when hot, add the chops and fry for 2 minutes on each side until browned (this can be done using the Sauté function in your Instant Pot, selecting More for a high heat, but you'll need to cook in two batches). If using a frying pan, transfer the chops to your Instant Pot when browned.

2   In a jug, blend together the orange juice, honey, soy sauce, sherry, vinegar, mustard and tomato purée with a little pepper. Pour about half over the chops, then turn the chops so that they are coated in the sauce. Pour over the rest of the sauce.

3   Put on the lid, lock into place and turn the pressure-release switch to Sealing. Press Manual (Pressure Cook), adjust the pressure to Low and the time to 1 minute.

4   After cooking, allow the pressure to release naturally for 10 minutes, then quick-release the remaining pressure. Serve straight away.

Chicken and Poultry

Chicken is always a firm favourite and the versatility of your Instant Pot means that there is something here for everyone, whether you want a simple roast, a tantalising warm and spicy curry, or an elegant dish with a delicate white wine and tarragon sauce.

Whatever cut you prefer – breasts, drumsticks or thighs – you'll discover recipes for them here. A little care needs to be taken with the leaner cuts and they are often best braised to keep them moist or cooked on low pressure. More robust thighs and drumsticks can be cooked until the meat is so tender it almost falls off the bones.

There's more than just chicken in this chapter though: your Instant Pot can also be used to cook other poultry, including turkey, guinea fowl and duck.

Herb and Garlic Pot-roast Chicken

It's easy to cook a whole chicken in your Instant Pot. It will remain moist during cooking and a flavoured butter will make it even more succulent and tasty.

SERVES 4

25g (1oz) butter, softened
15g (½oz) fresh coriander, chopped
15g (½oz) fresh parsley, chopped
2 cloves garlic, crushed
Salt and freshly ground black pepper
1 chicken, about 1.3kg (3lb), without giblets
250ml (8fl oz) water

1   Put the butter, coriander, parsley, garlic, salt and pepper in a bowl and mix. Place the chicken on a board, breast-side up. Very carefully ease your fingers under the skin, starting at the neck end. Loosen the skin over the breasts and thighs, without breaking it. Push the butter mixture under the skin, easing it out in a thin layer.

2   Put the trivet (steaming rack) in your Instant Pot and pour in the water. Put the chicken on the trivet, breast-side up.

3   Put on the lid and lock into place. Turn the pressure-release switch to Sealing. Press Poultry and adjust the pressure to High and the time to 25 minutes. After cooking, allow the pressure to release naturally. Unlock and remove the lid.

4   Carefully remove the chicken; it won't need 'resting' as this will have taken place when your Instant Pot depressurised. Transfer to a board, carve and serve straight away.

COOK'S NOTE
- Check the chicken is done by inserting a thin knife or skewer into the thickest part of the leg. The knife or skewer should be hot when removed, and the juices from the meat should run clear (not pink).

VARIATION
- For Lemon and Paprika Pot-roast Chicken, grate the zest from 1 lemon and mix with 10ml (2 tsp) smoked paprika, 25g (1oz) softened butter, salt and freshly ground black pepper. Cut the lemon in quarters and place in the cavity of the chicken, then push the flavoured butter under the chicken skin as in step 1. Follow steps 2–4 as main recipe.

Slow-braised Chicken in Smoky Bacon Sauce

Your Instant Pot Slow Cook function makes slightly tougher cuts of chicken beautifully tender, while retaining the shape and texture of vegetables and fruit such as apples. It's easier to brown the chicken legs in a large frying pan than in your Instant Pot as there will be more room to turn the meat.

SERVES 4

100g (4oz) smoked pancetta or bacon lardons
4 chicken legs
100g (4oz) baby button mushrooms
2 leeks, sliced
2 eating apples, quartered, cored and thickly sliced
10ml (2 tsp) chopped fresh thyme
300ml (½ pint) chicken stock, preferably home-made
   (page 44)
Salt and freshly ground black pepper

1 Heat a large non-stick frying pan, add the pancetta or bacon lardons and cook over a medium-high heat for 3–4 minutes or until lightly browned. Transfer to the inner pot using a slotted spoon, leaving all the fat behind.
2 Add the chicken legs to the frying pan and fry for a few minutes on both sides until well browned. Transfer to your Instant Pot, fitting them closely together.
3 Add the mushrooms and leeks to the frying pan and cook for a minute until lightly browned. Transfer to the pot with the apples and thyme. Pour over the stock and season with salt and pepper.

4   Put on the lid and lock into place. Turn the pressure-release switch to Venting. Press Slow Cook and adjust to Normal for a medium heat; the time will automatically set to 4 hours.

5   When cooking is complete, unlock and remove the lid and leave to stand for a couple of minutes. Skim any fat from the top before serving.

COOK'S NOTE
- If you want to thicken the gravy, press Sauté and adjust to More for a high heat. Transfer the chicken legs and some of the vegetables to a warmed serving dish using a slotted spoon. Blend 15ml (1 tbsp) cornflour with 15ml (1 tbsp) cold water and stir into the gravy. Let it bubble for a minute or two, stirring frequently, until it has thickened. Spoon the gravy over the meat and vegetables.

Sticky Chicken Drumsticks

Using your Instant Pot in combination with a grill creates drumsticks that are beautifully brown and sticky, yet still succulent and perfectly cooked.

SERVES 4

8 skin-on meaty chicken drumsticks
30ml (2 tbsp) chicken stock, preferably home-made
   (page 44), or water
60ml (4 tbsp) balsamic vinegar
30ml (2 tbsp) honey
15ml (1 tbsp) Dijon mustard
Salt and freshly ground black pepper
1.5ml (¼ tsp) dried thyme

1   Trim the drumsticks if necessary and remove any excess fat. Put the stock or water, vinegar, honey and mustard in your Instant Pot and stir together to combine.
2   Season the drumsticks with a little salt and pepper and add to the pot with the dried thyme, turning in the sauce to coat them all over.
3   Put on the lid and lock into place. Turn the pressure-release switch to Sealing. Press Manual (Pressure Cook), adjust the pressure to High and the time to 7 minutes. After cooking, allow the pressure to release naturally for 5 minutes, then quick-release the remaining pressure. Unlock and remove the lid.
4   While the pressure is releasing, line a grill pan with foil and preheat the grill to high. Carefully lift the drumsticks out of your Instant Pot using tongs and place on the grill pan. Grill for 3–5 minutes, turning frequently, until the skin is brown and crispy.
5   Press Sauté and adjust to Normal for a medium heat. Let the sauce bubble for a few minutes until reduced to a thick sticky glaze. Spoon a little over the chicken before serving.

Fragrant Spiced Chicken

This simple spiced dish with lentils and spinach has no added fat and uses skinned chicken thighs. The lentils will cook down completely to make a thick spicy sauce. This makes a great midweek meal served with plain white or brown basmati rice (see page 7).

SERVES 4

75g (3oz) red lentils
30ml (2 tbsp) mild curry paste, e.g. korma
300ml (½ pint) chicken stock, preferably home-made (page 44)
8 chicken thighs, skinned
Salt and freshly ground black pepper
125g (4½oz) bag baby spinach leaves
30ml (2 tbsp) chopped fresh coriander

1   Rinse the lentils in a sieve under cold running water, drain well and tip into your Instant Pot. Add the curry paste and about a third of the stock and stir to blend the curry paste. Add the chicken thighs and pour over the remaining stock. Season with salt and pepper.
2   Put on the lid and lock into place. Turn the pressure-release switch to Sealing. Press Poultry and adjust the pressure to High and the time to 12 minutes.
3   When cooking is complete, press Keep Warm/Cancel and allow the pressure to release naturally for 10 minutes. Quick-release any remaining pressure and remove the lid.
4   Stir in the baby spinach and coriander, cover with the lid and leave for a couple of minutes for the spinach to cook and wilt. Serve straight away.

COOK'S NOTE
- Commercial stock cubes often contain a lot of salt, as do curry pastes. If you are not using home-made stock, it is better to season this dish after cooking.

Chicken Jalfrezi

This tantalising curry always contains tomatoes and peppers. Chargrilling and skinning peppers is fiddly and time-consuming, so here a jar of ready-prepared ones is used instead. These are usually stored in oil, so drain well before using.

SERVES 4

30ml (2 tbsp) ghee or coconut oil (or use oil from the chargrilled pepper jar)
1 onion, chopped
2 cloves garlic, crushed
15ml (1 tbsp) Madras curry paste
15ml (1 tbsp) tomato purée
60ml (4 tbsp) vegetable stock, preferably home-made (page 45), or water
400g (14oz) can chopped tomatoes
5ml (1 tsp) balsamic vinegar
400g (14oz) chicken breasts, cut into bite-sized pieces
Salt and freshly ground black pepper
150g (5oz) chargrilled red peppers, sliced
Rice or naan bread, to serve

1   Preheat your Instant Pot by selecting Sauté and adjust to Normal for medium heat. Add the ghee or coconut oil and when it is hot, add the onion. Cook, stirring frequently, for 3–4 minutes until almost soft.
2   Add the garlic and curry paste and cook for a further 30 seconds, stirring all the time. Add the tomato purée and stock or water and stir until blended, then stir in the chopped tomatoes, balsamic vinegar and chicken. Season with salt and pepper. Cancel the Sauté function.

3 Put on the lid and lock into place. Turn the pressure-release switch to Sealing. Press Poultry, adjust the pressure to High and the time to 3 minutes. After cooking, allow the pressure to release naturally for 5 minutes, then quick-release the remaining pressure. Unlock and remove the lid.

4 Meanwhile, put the chargrilled peppers in a sieve and pour over some boiling water (about a quarter kettleful); this will remove some of the oil and heat the peppers at the same time. Tip into the chicken mixture and stir well. Serve straight away with rice (page 7) or warmed naan breads.

Creamy Chicken Korma

One of the mildest of classic Indian curries, korma sauces tend to be rich and creamy, usually with the addition of coconut milk and ground almonds. You can make this with chicken breast or with less-expensive chicken thighs.

SERVES 4

For the sauce
50g (2oz) blanched almonds or cashew nuts
1 small onion, roughly chopped
3 cloves garlic, halved
½ green chilli, seeds removed
15ml (1 tbsp) grated fresh ginger
5ml (1 tsp) garam masala
5ml (1 tsp) ground cumin
5ml (1 tsp) ground coriander
5ml (1 tsp) ground turmeric
2.5–5ml (½–1 tsp) salt
100ml (4fl oz) water

For the chicken
400g (14oz) skinless chicken breasts or boneless, skinless thighs
15ml (1 tbsp) tomato purée
75ml (5 tbsp) coconut milk
45ml (3 tbsp) chopped fresh coriander (optional)
50g (2oz) toasted flaked almonds or toasted cashew nuts, roughly chopped (optional), to garnish

1   For the sauce, put the nuts, onion, garlic, chilli, ginger, garam
    masala, cumin, coriander, turmeric, salt and water in a
    blender or food processor and blend to a smooth paste,
    stopping and scraping down the sides a couple of times.
2   Pour the sauce into your Instant Pot. If using chicken
    breasts, cut each into three pieces. Add the chicken to the
    sauce.
3   Put on the lid and lock into place. Turn the pressure-release
    switch to Sealing. Press Manual (Pressure Cook), adjust the
    pressure to High and the time to 8 minutes. After cooking,
    allow the pressure to release naturally. Unlock and remove
    the lid.
4   While the pressure is releasing, stir the tomato purée and
    coconut milk together. Remove the chicken from the sauce
    and place on warmed plates. Stir the coconut milk mixture
    and coriander, if using, into the sauce and spoon over the
    chicken. Scatter with flaked almonds or chopped cashew
    nuts, if liked.

COOK'S NOTES
- Make sure you use canned coconut milk (or reconstituted block
  coconut) and not coconut 'drinking' milk from a carton.
- This dish is good served with Cucumber Raita: Peel and grate
  1 medium-sized cucumber and place in a sieve, sprinkling
  between the layers with 2.5ml (½ tsp) salt (this draws out some
  of the juices so the yogurt isn't diluted too much). Leave over a
  bowl to drain for 20 minutes, then gently press down on the
  cucumber with the back of a spoon to squeeze out the juices.
  Tip the cucumber into a bowl and add 200ml (7fl oz) Greek
  Yogurt (page 30), 15ml (1 tbsp) chopped fresh coriander and
  15ml (1 tbsp) chopped fresh mint.

Paprika Chicken

This is a lower-fat version of *paprikash*, a popular Romanian dish. It's thickened after cooking, although you can leave the sauce thinner if you prefer. It's particularly good served on a bed of plain white or wholegrain rice (page 7).

SERVES 4

15ml (1 tbsp) sunflower oil
8 boneless, skinless chicken thighs
1 large onion, halved and finely sliced
1 clove garlic, crushed
15ml (1 tbsp) smoked paprika, plus extra to sprinkle
2 peppers, preferably one red and one yellow, halved, seeded and cut into 2cm (¾in) pieces
5ml (1 tsp) dried mixed herbs
1 bay leaf
400g (14oz) can chopped tomatoes
300ml (½ pint) chicken stock, preferably home-made (page 44)
Salt and freshly ground black pepper
10ml (2 tsp) cornflour
15ml (1 tbsp) cold water
Sour cream or Greek yogurt (page 30), to serve

1   Preheat your Instant Pot by selecting Sauté and adjust to Normal for medium heat. When hot, add the oil. Pat the chicken thighs dry on kitchen paper, then add to the pot and brown them for 2 minutes on each side. Transfer to a plate, retaining the oil in the pot, and set aside.

2   Add the onion to the pot and cook for 3–4 minutes or until almost soft, stirring frequently, adding a spoonful of stock if it starts to stick. Add the garlic and cook for a few more seconds. Cancel the Sauté function.

3   Sprinkle over the paprika and stir in, then add the peppers, dried herbs and bay leaf. Add the chopped tomatoes and stock. Season with salt and pepper and stir well. Return the chicken to the pot with any juices on the plate and push down into the sauce.

4   Put on the lid and lock into place. Turn the pressure-release switch to Sealing. Press Manual (Pressure Cook), adjust the pressure to High and the time to 10 minutes. After cooking, allow the pressure to release naturally for 10 minutes, then quick-release the remaining pressure. Unlock and remove the lid. Press Sauté and adjust to Less for a low heat.

5   Blend the cornflour and cold water together. Stir into the sauce and simmer for 3–4 minutes until thickened. Cancel the Sauté function. Serve on warmed plates, topping each with a spoonful of sour cream or Greek yogurt and a sprinkling of smoked paprika.

Tarragon Chicken in White Wine

Here, chicken is served in a wine and crème fraiche sauce with little button onions to make an elegant dish, ideal for entertaining. Tarragon has a distinctive, almost aniseed, flavour that goes particularly well with chicken.

SERVES 4

225g (8oz) small button onions
15g (½oz) unsalted butter
30ml (2 tbsp) sunflower oil
4 boneless chicken breast portions, skinned
200ml (7fl oz) dry white wine
150ml (¼ pint) chicken stock, preferably home-made (page 44)
Salt and freshly ground black pepper
5ml (1 tsp) cornflour
150ml (¼ pint) crème fraiche
45ml (3 tbsp) chopped fresh tarragon

1 Put the onions in a heatproof bowl and pour over enough boiling water to cover the onions by about 5cm (2in). Leave to stand for 10 minutes, then drain and peel off the skins; the onions should be beginning to soften and the skins should slip off easily.
2 Preheat your Instant Pot by selecting Sauté and adjust to Normal for medium heat. Add the butter and 15ml (1 tbsp) of the oil and when the butter has melted, add the onions and cook for 4–5 minutes, stirring frequently, until the onions are golden-brown all over. Remove from the pot and set aside.

3 Add the remaining 15ml (1 tbsp) of oil to the pot and allow it to heat (or the chicken will stick). Pat the chicken breasts dry on kitchen paper, then add two to your Instant Pot and sauté for 1–2 minutes each side, until golden. Remove from the pot and transfer to a plate. Repeat with the remaining two chicken breasts (if you prefer, you can brown the chicken breasts in one go in a large non-stick frying pan).

4 Return the onions to the pot and pour in the white wine. Bring to the boil and simmer for 2 minutes to allow the alcohol to evaporate and the flavour to concentrate (at this stage the onions should be almost tender). Pour in the chicken stock, then cancel the Sauté function. Season with salt and pepper, then add the chicken breasts, pushing them down into the sauce as far as possible.

5 Put on the lid and lock into place. Turn the pressure-release switch to Sealing. Press Poultry, adjust the pressure to Low and the time to 10 minutes. After cooking, naturally release the pressure for 10 minutes, then quick-release any remaining pressure. Unlock and remove the lid.

6 While the pressure is releasing, blend the cornflour with the crème fraiche and tarragon. Press Sauté and adjust to Less for a low heat. Remove the chicken breasts from the pot, transfer to a warm plate, cover with foil and keep warm. Stir the crème fraiche mixture into the sauce. Let the sauce bubble for a minute or two, then cancel the Sauté function. Serve the chicken and onions on warmed plates with the sauce spooned over.

Turkey Mole

Mole is a classic spicy Mexican dish with a thick dark sauce containing chillies and a little dark chocolate, which enriches it and gives the dish a rounded mellow flavour. It can be very hot, but this version is fairly mild.

SERVES 4

30ml (2 tbsp) sunflower oil
1 large onion, chopped
2 cloves garlic, crushed
30ml (2 tbsp) sesame seeds
450g (1lb) skinless turkey breast, cut into 2cm (¾in) cubes
15ml (1 tbsp) mild chilli powder
1.5ml (¼ tsp) ground mixed spice
400g (14oz) can chopped tomatoes
150ml (¼ pint) chicken stock, preferably home-made
    (page 44)
50g (2oz) raisins (optional)
Salt and freshly ground black pepper
25g (1oz) dark chocolate, roughly chopped
60ml (4 tbsp) toasted flaked almonds
45ml (3 tbsp) chopped fresh coriander

1   Preheat your Instant Pot by selecting Sauté and adjust to Normal for a medium heat. Add the oil and when it is hot, add the onion. Cook for 3–4 minutes, stirring frequently, until beginning to soften. Add the garlic and sesame seeds and cook for a further 3–4 minutes, until the onion is soft and beginning to colour.

2   Stir in the turkey, then sprinkle over the chilli powder and
    mixed spice and stir until coated. Add the tomatoes, chicken
    stock and raisins, if using. Season with salt and pepper and
    stir well.
3   Put on the lid and lock into place. Turn the pressure-release
    switch to Sealing. Press Manual (Pressure Cook), adjust the
    pressure to High and the time to 8 minutes. After cooking,
    allow the pressure to release naturally for 8 minutes, then
    quick-release the remaining pressure. Unlock and remove
    the lid.
4   Scatter the chocolate over the sauce and stir until melted.
    Stir in 30ml (2 tbsp) of the almonds and 30ml (2 tbsp) of the
    chopped coriander. Spoon onto warmed plates and serve
    straight away, scattered with the remaining almonds and
    coriander.

Orange and Ginger Duck

Duck breast is a good source of iron and zinc. Here, it is marinated to tenderise and flavour the meat (you can cut out this step if you are in a hurry), then briefly sautéed before being cut into thick slices.

SERVES 4

4 oranges
Squeezed juice from finely grated 2.5cm (1in) piece fresh
  ginger
4 duck breasts, about 500g (14oz) in total
15ml (1 tbsp) sunflower oil
1 clove garlic, crushed
4 spring onions, trimmed and finely sliced
30ml (2 tbsp) soy sauce
15ml (1 tbsp) sherry vinegar
100ml (4fl oz) chicken stock, preferably home-made (page 44)
1 bay leaf
Salt and freshly ground black pepper
5ml (1 tsp) cornflour
15ml (1 tbsp) chopped fresh mint

1 Finely grate the zest from one of the oranges and squeeze the
   juice from two. Put the zest and juice in a shallow dish.
   Remove the skin and fat from the duck and add the duck to
   the dish, turning to coat in juice. If you have time, cover and
   leave to marinate for an hour at room temperature or
   overnight in the fridge.
2 Remove the duck from the marinade and pat dry on kitchen
   paper. Preheat your Instant Pot by selecting Sauté and adjust to
   More for a high heat. Add the oil and when heated, add the duck
   breasts and cook for 1 minute on each side, until browned. (You
   will need to do this in two batches.) Remove and place on a
   chopping board. Cancel the Sauté setting.

3   Press Sauté again and adjust to Less for a low heat. Add the garlic and spring onions and cook for about 30 seconds until beginning to soften, then pour in the orange marinade, soy sauce, vinegar and chicken stock. Cut the duck breasts, on the diagonal, into 1.5cm (½in) thick slices. Add to the pot with the bay leaf, salt and pepper. Stir, then cancel the Sauté setting.

4   Put on the lid and lock into place. Turn the pressure-release switch to Sealing. Press Manual (Pressure Cook), adjust the pressure to High and the time to 2 minutes. After cooking, allow the pressure to release naturally for 5 minutes, then quick-release the remaining pressure. Unlock and remove the lid.

5   While the duck is cooking, peel the remaining two oranges, removing all the white pith, then cut between the membranes to remove the orange segments. Squeeze out any juice from the membranes and orange peel and blend the juice with the cornflour.

6   Stir the blended cornflour into the duck mixture. It should still be hot enough to thicken; if not, press Sauté and adjust to Less until it comes back to the boil. Stir in the orange segments and mint and serve straight away.

VARIATION
- For Pink Grapefruit and Honey Duck, finely grate 10ml (2 tsp) zest and squeeze the juice from one pink grapefruit and use to marinate the duck in step 1. Follow steps 2–4 in the main recipe, adding 15ml (1 tbsp) honey with the grapefruit marinade in step 3. In step 5, segment two pink grapefruit and complete following the rest of the recipe.

Guinea Fowl and Spring Vegetable Braise

Guinea fowl is now available all year round. It's not as big as chicken, so you'll need two birds to serve four. Although it is typically paired with red cabbage and chestnuts, it's equally delicious with more delicate flavourings such as spring vegetables. The meat really benefits from long, moist cooking, as shown here.

SERVES 4

2 guinea fowl, about 1.2kg (2lb 12oz) each
30ml (2 tbsp) plain flour
Salt and freshly ground black pepper
30ml (2 tbsp) sunflower oil
2 cloves garlic, crushed
150ml (¼ pint) dry white wine
10ml (2 tsp) wholegrain mustard
225g (8oz) baby carrots
225g (8oz) baby turnips
8 baby leeks, cut into 7.5cm (3in) lengths
1 sprig fresh rosemary
1 bay leaf
200ml (7fl oz) chicken or vegetable stock, preferably home-
  made (pages 44–45)
150g (5oz) frozen peas, defrosted
30ml (2 tbsp) chopped fresh parsley
30ml (2 tbsp) chopped fresh mint

1 To joint the guinea fowl (or you can ask the butcher to do
   this for you), bend the legs and thighs away from the birds,
   then cut between the joint to separate them. Cut between the
   thigh and leg joints to make two pieces, then cut off the
   wings. Cut either side of the breastbone to remove the
   breasts. Remove the skin from all the pieces of meat.

2 Mix the flour with a little salt and pepper and use to lightly dust the meat. Heat the oil in a large non-stick frying pan over a high heat, add the meat and fry for a minute or two, turning frequently, until golden brown. (If you prefer, do this in batches, using the Sauté function in your Instant Pot).

3 Transfer the guinea fowl to your Instant Pot, leaving any fat and juices in the frying pan. Add the garlic to the frying pan and cook for a few seconds, then pour in the white wine. Let it bubble for a minute or two, scraping any sediment from the bottom of the frying pan, then pour over the guinea fowl.

4 Add the carrots, turnips, leeks, rosemary and bay leaf to your Instant Pot, then pour over the stock. Season with salt and pepper.

5 Put on the lid and lock into place. Turn the pressure-release switch to Venting. Press Slow Cook and adjust to Normal for a medium heat. The time should automatically set to 4 hours.

6 When cooking is complete, remove the lid. Put the peas in a sieve and pour over boiling water to heat them, then stir into the casserole with the chopped parsley and mint. Serve straight away.

COOK'S NOTE
- Use the wings and carcass to make stock, following the recipe for chicken stock on page 44.

5

Fish and Seafood

The perfect healthy choice for all kinds of tempting dishes, fish and seafood are a great source of protein and provide many vitamins and minerals. White fish is low in fat; oily fish such as salmon is a great source of heart-healthy polyunsaturated fatty acids such as omega-3.

Although large whole fish may be too big for your Instant Pot, it's perfect for fish steaks and fillets and great if you want to cook seafood, such as prawns, from frozen. Fish and seafood cook really quickly in your Instant Pot, so you do need to take care not to overcook them. Steaming, cooking on low pressure and slow-simmering with your Sauté function are often the best ways to cook these delicate foods.

As well as the array of fish dishes in this chapter, you'll also find recipes elsewhere in the book, so do have a look in the index. Try Smoked Salmon and Avocado Kedgeree (page 26) for breakfast or Creole-style Prawn Gumbo (page 180) if you want to spice up your seafood.

Teriyaki Steamed Salmon

For maximum flavour, marinate the salmon for at least 10 minutes at room temperature or preferably several hours in the fridge. It is better to choose small thick salmon fillets than large thin ones, as they will fit better in your Instant Pot.

SERVES 4

4 salmon fillets, about 125g (4½oz) each
15ml (1 tbsp) sweet chilli sauce
15ml (1 tbsp) mirin or dry sherry
15ml (1 tbsp) dark soy sauce
15ml (1 tbsp) finely grated fresh ginger
250ml (8fl oz) water
15ml (1 tbsp) toasted sesame seeds, for sprinkling

1 Put the salmon fillets in a shallow dish. Mix together the chilli sauce, mirin or sherry, soy sauce and ginger, and spoon over the tops and sides of the fillets. Cover and marinate at room temperature for up to 30 minutes or in the fridge for a few hours.

2 Place the steaming rack (trivet) in the inner pot and pour in the water. Arrange the salmon fillets on top. Try to place in a single layer, but if necessary, overlap the thinner parts of salmon.

3 Put on the lid and lock into place. Turn the pressure-release switch to Sealing. Press Steam, adjust to the Normal setting and the time to 5 minutes.

4 After cooking, quick-release the steam and remove the lid. Carefully lift out the salmon and sprinkle with toasted sesame seeds before serving.

COOK'S NOTE

- The timing is based on fillets that are about 2.5cm (1in) thick. Adjust if you have thicker or thinner fillets, adding or deducting 1 minute for every 5mm (¼in) e.g. 2cm (¾in) fillets will take 4 minutes, and 4cm (1½in) fillets will take 7 minutes.

Fish and Vegetable Dim Sum

These steamed dumplings are made with wonton wrappers, which you can buy in Chinese grocers and some large supermarkets. Filled with a mixture of finely chopped white fish and vegetables, they are delicious served with a simple dipping sauce.

SERVES 4 (MAKES 20)

15ml (1 tbsp) sesame or sunflower oil
15ml (1 tbsp) finely grated fresh ginger
1 clove garlic, crushed
1 small carrot, finely chopped
2 spring onions, trimmed and finely chopped
50g (2oz) baby spinach leaves, finely shredded
225g (8oz) piece skinless white fish, such as cod
1 medium egg white
10ml (2 tsp) cornflour
Salt, to taste
20 wonton wrappers, 9cm (3½in) size
250ml (8fl oz) water

To serve
Sweet chilli sauce or soy dipping sauce made by mixing 30ml
   (2 tbsp) soy sauce with 30ml (2 tbsp) sherry

1   Preheat your Instant Pot by pressing Sauté and adjust to
    Normal for medium heat. Add the oil and when hot, add the
    ginger, garlic, carrot and spring onions. Cook, stirring
    frequently, for 3–4 minutes until almost soft. Cancel the
    Sauté function, add the spinach leaves and cook in the
    residual heat until wilted and all the excess liquid has
    evaporated. Tip onto a plate and leave to cool for a few
    minutes (spread out the mixture, so that it cools more
    quickly). Wipe the pot clean with kitchen paper.

2 Chop the fish very finely (do this in a food processor if you prefer). Lightly whisk the egg white and cornflour together in a bowl, add the fish and mix well. Add the vegetable mixture, season with a little salt (not too much if you are serving with a soy dipping sauce) and mix everything together.

3 To make the dim sum, spoon a teaspoon of fish mixture into the middle of a wonton wrapper. Dampen the edges with a little water, then bring up the sides of the wrapper around the filling, pinching the edges together at the top to seal. Try to shape them so they are tall and thin rather than short and squat, so that they will fit into your Instant Pot in two batches. Repeat with the remaining filling and wrappers.

4 Pour the water into your Instant Pot and add the trivet (steaming rack). Arrange 10 of the dim sum on the rack. Put on the lid and lock into place. Turn the pressure-release switch to Sealing. Press Steam, adjust the setting to Normal and the time to 5 minutes.

5 After cooking, quick-release the pressure and remove the lid. Transfer the dim sum to a warmed plate and cover loosely with foil. Cook the remaining 10 dim sum in the same way. Serve straight away with a dipping sauce.

VARIATIONS

- For Fish and Vegetable Spring Rolls, use 8 spring roll wrappers. Divide the fish mixture into 8 and shape each into a small log about 8cm (3in) long. Follow the spring roll wrapper packet instructions, soaking them one at a time for about 3 seconds in warm water. Place the filling in the middle, fold over the sides, then fold over one of the edges. Roll up and place on the trivet (steaming rack), lightly oiling it first. Try to position them so that they are not touching each other or they will stick together. Follow step 4 to cook the spring rolls.

- For Prawn and Pork Dim Sum, make in the same way, but substitute 100g (4oz) prawns (defrost well and pat dry with kitchen paper, if using frozen) and 100g (4oz) minced pork for the white fish.

Monkfish Thai Green Curry

Look for packs of Thai spices that include lemongrass, galangal and lime leaves rather than buying the individual ingredients. Any firm white fish can be used for this dish, such as cod, hake or halibut.

SERVES 4

For the green curry paste
75ml (5 tbsp) chopped fresh coriander
30ml (2 tbsp) grated fresh galangal
10ml (2 tsp) chopped fresh lemongrass
3 lime leaves, chopped
4 shallots, roughly chopped
2 cloves garlic, peeled and halved
1 red chilli, halved and seeded
5ml (1 tsp) ground cumin
5ml (1 tsp) ground coriander
Grated zest of 1 lime
30ml (2 tbsp) fish sauce (nam pla)

For the monkfish curry
15ml (1 tbsp) sunflower oil
450ml (¾ pint) vegetable stock, preferably home-made (page 45)
15ml (1 tbsp) caster sugar
225g (8oz) even-sized new potatoes, scrubbed and quartered
450g (1lb) monkfish, cut across into 2cm (¾in) thick slices
100g (4oz) mangetout
100ml (4fl oz) coconut milk
Juice of 1 lime

1 For the green curry paste, reserve 45ml (3 tbsp) of the chopped coriander. Put the rest and all other ingredients for the green curry paste into a small food processor or blender. Add 60ml (4 tbsp) water and blend to a fairly smooth paste, stopping a couple of times and scraping down the sides.
2 For the monkfish curry, preheat your Instant Pot by selecting Sauté and adjust to Less for a low heat. Add the oil and when it is hot, pour in the green curry paste. Cook for 3–4 minutes, stirring frequently, especially towards the end of cooking time, until all the water has evaporated. Cancel Sauté and stir in the vegetable stock, sugar and potatoes.
3 Put on the lid and lock into place. Turn the pressure-release switch to Sealing. Press Manual (Pressure Cook), adjust the pressure to High and the time to 8 minutes. After cooking, quick-release the pressure. Unlock and remove the lid.
4 Press Sauté again and adjust to Less for a low heat. Stir in the monkfish, mangetout and coconut milk. Cover with a lid and cook for about 5 minutes or until the fish flakes easily and the mangetout are just tender.
5 Cancel the Sauté function. Stir in the lime juice and the reserved 30ml (2 tbsp) chopped fresh coriander and serve straight away on warm plates.

COOK'S NOTE
- Galangal is a knobbly-looking root from the ginger family and is prepared and used in exactly the same way as fresh ginger. If you can't get galangal, fresh ginger can be substituted.

Mediterranean Fish Stew with Crispy Croutons

Full of flavour, this delicious fish dish can be made using whatever is tasty and fresh from the sea. Little crunchy croutons sizzled in some good olive oil are a lovely finishing touch.

SERVES 4

For the croutons
30ml (2 tbsp) olive oil
3 slices granary bread, crusts removed and cut into small cubes

For the fish stew
30ml (2 tbsp) olive oil
1 medium onion, halved and finely sliced
2 cloves garlic, finely chopped
450g (1lb) new potatoes, cut into small chunks
5ml (1 tsp) paprika
400g (14oz) can chopped tomatoes
200ml (7fl oz) vegetable stock, preferably home-made (page 45)
1 sprig fresh thyme
1 sprig fresh rosemary
Freshly ground black pepper
200g (7oz) raw peeled king prawns, defrosted if frozen
400g (14oz) can chickpeas, drained and rinsed, or 250g (9oz) cooked chickpeas (page 8)
400g (14oz) skinless fish fillets, cut into large chunks
50g (2oz) stoned green olives

1   For the croutons, preheat your Instant Pot by pressing Sauté
    and adjust to More for high heat. When hot, add the oil and
    allow it to heat for a few seconds, then add the bread cubes.
    Cook for 3–4 minutes, stirring all the time until crisp and
    browned. Remove and set aside on a plate lined with kitchen
    paper. Press Keep Warm/Cancel.

2   For the fish stew, press Sauté and adjust to Normal for
    medium heat. Add the oil and when hot, add the onion and
    cook for 3–4 minutes, stirring frequently, then add the garlic,
    potatoes and paprika and cook for a futher minute. Pour in
    the chopped tomatoes and vegetable stock. Add the thyme
    and rosemary and season with black pepper.

3   Put on the lid and lock into place. Turn the pressure-release
    switch to Sealing. Press Manual (Pressure Cook), adjust the
    pressure to High and the time to 4 minutes. After cooking,
    quick-release the pressure. Unlock and remove the lid.

4   Press Sauté and adjust to Normal for medium heat. Stir in
    the prawns, chickpeas, fish and olives. Cover with a pan lid
    and cook for 5–6 minutes, stirring once or twice. When the
    fish and prawns are just cooked through, cancel the Sauté
    function. Remove the thyme and rosemary stalks (the leaves
    will have fallen off into the stew). Serve in warmed bowls,
    scattering over the croutons just before serving.

Garlic Mussels in White Wine

Mussels only take minutes to cook on the hob, but steaming them in your Instant Pot locks in their fresh seafood flavour and keeps them succulent.

SERVES 4

5ml (1 tsp) olive oil
15g (½oz) butter
2 shallots, finely chopped
2 cloves garlic, crushed
150ml (¼ pint) dry white wine
1kg (2¼lb) mussels in shells, cleaned
60ml (4 tbsp) double cream or crème fraiche
30ml (2 tbsp) chopped fresh parsley
Freshly ground black pepper

1 Preheat your Instant Pot by pressing Sauté and adjust to Normal for a medium heat. When the inner pot is hot, add the oil and butter. When the butter is sizzling, add the shallots and cook for 3–4 minutes until almost soft, stirring frequently. Add the garlic and cook for a few more seconds, then pour in the wine.
2 Bring the wine to the boil and let it bubble for about 30 seconds, to allow the alcohol to evaporate. Tip in all the mussels. Put on the lid and lock into place. Turn the pressure-release switch to Sealing. Press Manual (Pressure Cook), adjust the pressure to High and the time to 1 minute.

3 After cooking, allow the pressure to release naturally for 2 minutes, then quick-release the remaining pressure. Unlock and remove the lid.

4 Tip the mussels into a colander over a bowl and discard any that haven't opened. Cover the colander with foil to keep the mussels warm. Rinse out the inner pot (there may be one or two specks of grit), then strain the cooking liquid back into the pot through a muslin-lined sieve.

5 Press Sauté and adjust to Normal for a medium heat. Add the cream or crème fraiche and parsley to the pan and season with black pepper. Heat until steaming hot and just starting to boil. Meanwhile, divide the mussels between warmed bowls. Pour over the sauce and serve straight away.

COOK'S NOTE
- When preparing mussels, discard any with cracked or broken shells and any that do not close when tapped. Scrape any barnacles off the shells and pull out the thread-like 'beards'. Rinse the mussels several times in cold water.

Smoked Salmon and Haddock Terrine

Layers of pink and white fish are studded with capers in this attractive terrine. It makes a wonderful light lunch accompanied by a fresh dill and lime mayonnaise. Make sure that your loaf tin will comfortably fit in your Instant Pot before you start.

SERVES 4

200g (7oz) smoked salmon
675g (1½lb) haddock fillets, skinned
1 medium egg
1 medium egg white
75ml (5 tbsp) crème fraiche or sour cream
15ml (1 tbsp) capers, drained
Salt and white pepper

For the dill and lime mayonnaise
120ml (8 tbsp) mayonnaise (low-fat, if preferred)
10ml (2 tsp) finely grated lime zest
15ml (1 tbsp) lime juice
30ml (2 tbsp) snipped fresh dill

1   Use about two-thirds of the smoked salmon to line a 750ml (1¼ pint) loaf tin, allowing the ends of the salmon to hang over the sides of the tin (they'll be folded in later).
2   Cut the haddock into small cubes about 1cm (½in) in size. Whisk the egg and egg white in a bowl using a fork, then mix in the crème fraiche, capers, salt and pepper. Add the haddock and mix well. Spoon half of the haddock mixture into the tin.

3 Lay about half of the remaining salmon on top (don't worry if there are big gaps, just space it out evenly), then spoon in the remaining haddock mixture. Fold the overhanging pieces of smoked salmon over the top, patching any gaps with the final pieces of smoked salmon (it doesn't matter if you don't have enough to cover all of the haddock mixture). Tightly cover the tin with a double thickness of foil.

4 Put the trivet (steaming rack) in the bottom of the inner pot and place the tin on top. Carefully pour in enough hot water to come just over halfway up the side of the tin. Put on the lid and lock into place. Press Slow Cook, adjust to More for high heat and the time to 1¾ hours.

5 Unlock and remove the lid. Carefully lift the terrine out of your Instant Pot. Check that the terrine is cooked by inserting a skewer into the middle; it should come out hot and clean. Return the foil covering to the top of the terrine and weight it down by placing a can on top, e.g. a can of soup or tomatoes. Leave until cold, then chill in the fridge for at least 4 hours, or overnight, if preferred.

6 To make the dill and lime mayonnaise, put all the ingredients in a small bowl and mix together.

7 Turn out the terrine and cut into slices using a sharp knife. Serve with the flavoured mayonnaise.

Fish Balls in Tomato Sauce

These tasty little nuggets are rather like fish fingers without the crumb coating and will be enjoyed by children and adults alike. Easy to make, they are simmered in a smooth tomato sauce and are delicious on a bed of rice, noodles or pasta.

SERVES 4

400ml (14fl oz) passata
5ml (1 tsp) vegetable bouillon powder or ½ vegetable
   stock cube
2.5ml (½ tsp) dried mixed herbs
15ml (1 tbsp) soy sauce
450g (1lb) white fish fillets, skinned
15g (½oz) white or wholemeal breadcrumbs
Salt and white pepper

1 Pour the passata into your inner pot. Add the bouillon powder or stock cube (crumbled if a 'dry' cube), herbs and soy sauce. Press Sauté and adjust to Less for a low heat. As it comes up to simmering point, give it a stir to mix in the bouillon or stock cube. When it starts to bubble, cancel the Sauté function.

2 Meanwhile, cut the fish into chunks and put in a food processor with the breadcrumbs. Season with a little salt and pepper. Process the mixture until it is very finely chopped, but not completely smooth.

3 Divide the mixture into 20 even-sized pieces, then with slightly damp hands to stop the mixture sticking, shape each into a small ball. Carefully place the fish balls in the sauce.

4 Put on the lid and lock into place. Press Manual (Pressure Cook) and adjust the pressure to High and the time to 1 minute. After cooking, allow the pressure to release naturally for 5 minutes, then quick-release the remaining pressure. Unlock and remove the lid and serve straight away.

COOK'S NOTE
- If you are making this dish for adults, jazz up the sauce with your favourite seasoning, such as a pinch of dried chilli flakes or chopped herbs such as chives or parsley (if using fresh herbs, stir in after cooking).

Haddock with Braised Puy Lentils

Here, your Instant Pot is initially used as a slow cooker to slow-braise the lentils, then as a pressure cooker to quickly steam the fish to perfection – the best of both worlds.

SERVES 4

For the lentils
10ml (2 tsp) olive oil
50g (2oz) pancetta or smoked streaky bacon (rind removed), chopped
1 red onion, finely chopped
1 stick celery, finely chopped
2 cloves garlic, finely chopped
350g (12oz) Puy lentils
1 sprig fresh rosemary
750ml (1¼ pints) vegetable stock, preferably home-made (page 45)
Salt and freshly ground black pepper
5ml (1 tsp) red wine vinegar

For the haddock
15g (½oz) butter, softened
10ml (1 tsp) lemon juice
5ml (1 tsp) finely grated lemon zest
4 thick 150g (5oz) pieces of haddock fillet or steak

1   Preheat your Instant Pot by pressing Sauté and adjust to Normal for medium heat. Add the olive oil and when hot, add the pancetta or bacon. Cook for 2–3 minutes, stirring, until lightly browned. Remove from the pot with a slotted spoon, leaving the fat behind, and set aside.

2   Add the onion to the pot and cook for 2–3 minutes, stirring frequently. Add the celery and garlic and cook for a further 30 seconds, then return the pancetta to the pot. Cancel the Sauté function.

3   Rinse the lentils in a sieve under cold running water and tip into the pot. Add the rosemary and stock and season with salt and pepper. Put on the lid and lock into place. Press Slow Cook, adjust to More for a high heat and the time to 1 hour.

4   Meanwhile, blend the butter with the lemon juice and zest and a little salt and pepper. Dot on top of the fish. Remove the lid of your Instant Pot, stir in the vinegar and discard the rosemary. Place the fish, skin-side down, on top of the lentils.

5   Replace the lid and lock into place. Press Manual (Pressure Cook), adjust the pressure to Low and the time to 1 minute. After cooking, allow the pressure to release naturally for 5 minutes, then quick-release the remaining pressure. Unlock and remove the lid. Spoon the lentils and fish onto warmed plates and serve straight away.

Parma-wrapped Lemon Sole

Sole is a very delicate fish and cooks quickly. Filling with a moist stuffing and wrapping with Parma ham protects it during cooking. The fish is steamed over stock and wine, which is turned into a light-tasting sauce to serve with the fish.

SERVES 4

40g (1½oz) chopped toasted walnuts
40g (1½oz) fresh white breadcrumbs
15ml (1 tbsp) chopped fresh parsley
Salt and freshly ground black pepper
1 medium egg, lightly beaten
8 very thin slices Parma ham, about 125g (4½oz) in total, trimmed of fat
4 lemon sole fillets, about 150g (5oz) each, skinned
60ml (4 tbsp) dry white wine
60ml (4 tbsp) vegetable stock, preferably home-made (page 45)
5ml (1 tsp) cornflour

1   Put the walnuts, breadcrumbs and parsley in a bowl with a little salt and pepper. Add the egg and mix well.
2   Lay two overlapping slices of Parma ham on a board. Place a fish fillet on top, skinned side up. Spread a quarter of the walnut mixture over the fish, pressing it down lightly. Starting at the thicker end of the fillet, carefully roll up the fish and Parma ham to enclose the filling. Secure with wooden cocktail sticks. Repeat with the remaining ham, fish and filling.

3 Pour the wine and stock into the inner pot and put the steaming rack (trivet) in the pot. Place the fish rolls on the trivet, seam-side down.

4 Put on the lid and lock into place. Press Manual (Pressure Cook) and adjust the pressure to Low and the time to 3 minutes. After cooking, allow the pressure to release naturally for 3 minutes, then quick-release the remaining pressure. Unlock and remove the lid. Lift out the fish, cover with foil and keep warm.

5 Blend the cornflour with 10ml (2 tsp) of cold water and stir into the wine and stock mixture. Press Sauté and adjust to Normal for a medium heat. Let the sauce bubble for a minute, stirring until thickened. Spoon over the fish and serve straight away.

Simple Steamed Cod

Sometimes the simplest dishes are the best. Here flaky cod fillets are topped with a little caper butter and matchstick-cut vegetables and steamed for a light, healthy meal.

SERVES 4

150ml (¼ pint) vegetable stock, preferably home-made (page 45)
4 spring onions, trimmed and finely sliced
4 thick cod fillets, 175–200g (6–7oz) each
25g (1oz) butter, softened
30ml (2 tbsp) capers, drained and roughly chopped
5ml (1 tsp) finely grated lemon zest
Freshly ground black pepper
1 medium carrot
100g (4oz) mangetout

1 Pour the stock into your Instant Pot, add the spring onions, then place a trivet (steaming rack) in the pot.
2 Place the cod fillets on top of the trivet. Blend the butter, capers, lemon zest and black pepper together and dot over the top of the cod.
3 Cut the carrot into 5cm (2in) lengths, then cut into matchstick strips. Cut each mangetout in half lengthways. Scatter the vegetables over the fish.
4 Put on the lid and lock into place. Select Manual (Pressure Cook), adjust the pressure to Low and the time to 2 minutes. After cooking, quick-release the pressure. Unlock and remove the lid.
5 Carefully lift out the trivet and transfer the fish and vegetables to warmed plates. Spoon a little of the cooking liquid and spring onions over each and serve straight away.

6

Beans, Grains and Pasta

Cereal grains and pulses are the stars of the Instant Pot and take a fraction of the time they would to cook conventionally. There's a huge array to choose from that can be turned into many different dishes. Relatively inexpensive, they are also highly nutritious, which is great – especially if you follow a vegetarian or vegan diet.

Your Instant Pot has a special rice function which can sense how much rice has been added and will cook it to perfection with almost no effort on your part (see pages 7–8 in the Introduction for instructions and cooking times for all types of rice, grains and pulses).

Pasta is a great staple and brilliant for midweek meals. This chapter features pasta dishes from ever-popular Mac & Cheese to Creamy Tomato and Chorizo Penne, and Mushroom and Courgette Pasta, all one-pot meals made with the minimum of fuss.

Rich Lentil Ragu

This rich lentil and vegetable sauce is an excellent vegan answer
to minced beef bolognaise. Serve with pasta and freshly grated
vegan Parmesan-style cheese.

SERVES 4

150g (5oz) green lentils (lentilles vertes)
30ml (2 tbsp) olive oil
2 red onions, finely chopped
2 carrots, finely chopped
2 sticks celery, finely chopped
2 cloves garlic, crushed
5ml (1 tsp) dried oregano
1 sprig fresh rosemary (optional)
1 bay leaf
Pinch of sugar
300ml (½ pint) vegetable stock, preferably home-made
   (page 45)
150ml (¼ pint) full-bodied red wine or extra stock
400g (14oz) can chopped tomatoes
Salt and freshly ground black pepper

1 Thoroughly rinse the lentils and tip into a bowl. Cover with
   cold water and leave to soak for a few minutes while you
   prepare the rest of the ingredients.
2 Preheat your Instant Pot by selecting Sauté and adjust to
   Normal for medium heat. Add the olive oil to the inner pot
   and heat for a minute, then add the onions and cook, stirring
   frequently, for 3 minutes. Add the carrots and celery and
   cook for 2 minutes, stirring occasionally, then add the garlic
   and stir for a further minute. Cancel the Sauté function.

3 Drain the lentils and add to the pot with the oregano, rosemary, if using, bay leaf, sugar, stock, wine or extra stock and the tomatoes. Season with salt and pepper and stir well.

4 Put on the lid and lock into place. Select Manual (Pressure Cook) and turn the pressure-release switch to Sealing. Adjust the pressure to High and the time to 10 minutes. After cooking, allow the pressure to release naturally for 10 minutes, then quick-release any remaining pressure. Unlock and remove the lid. Remove the rosemary and bay leaf.

5 Season to taste with a little more salt and pepper if needed, then serve on top of freshly cooked pasta in warmed bowls. Finish with a generous sprinkling of freshly grated vegan Parmesan-style cheese.

Mac & Cheese

Pasta is popular for a quick midweek meal and this creamy version of macaroni cheese is easy to make in your Instant Pot. It uses both Cheddar and Gruyère cheese, but you can use all Cheddar if you prefer.

SERVES 4

350g (12oz) macaroni pasta
750ml (1¼ pints) boiling water
Pinch of salt
410g (14oz) can reduced-fat evaporated milk
5ml (1 tsp) English mustard powder
75g (3oz) mature Cheddar cheese, grated
50g (2oz) Gruyère cheese (or extra Cheddar), grated
Freshly ground black pepper

1 Put the macaroni in your Instant Pot and add the water and salt. Put on the lid, lock into place and turn the pressure-release switch to Sealing. Select Manual (Pressure Cook) and adjust the pressure to High and the time to 2 minutes.
2 After cooking is complete, press the Keep Warm/Cancel button. Allow the pressure to release naturally for 5 minutes, then quick-release the remaining pressure (do this carefully, as it may splutter a little). Remove the lid, give the pasta a stir to separate the pieces, then drain in a colander (the pasta will be slightly undercooked at this stage).
3 Press the Sauté button and adjust to Normal for a medium heat. Pour in the evaporated milk and add the mustard powder. Stir together until blended. Tip the pasta back into the pot and bring to the boil.

4   Let the pasta simmer, stirring frequently to separate the
    macaroni and prevent it sticking to the pot, for 2–3 minutes
    until the sauce thickens. It will look very thin at first, but will
    suddenly start to thicken as the pasta absorbs the sauce.
    Cancel Sauté and let it cook for a further minute in the
    residual heat, still stirring.
5   Stir in the cheese a handful at a time until melted and season
    with freshly ground black pepper. Serve straight away in
    warmed bowls.

COOK'S NOTE
- Cancel the Sauté function before the sauce reaches the desired
  thickness, as the pasta will continue to soak up the sauce for a
  few minutes. The cheese will further thicken the sauce.

VARIATIONS
- For Bacon and Tomato Pasta, snip 4 rashers smoked streaky
  bacon into small pieces using kitchen scissors. Put in the inner
  pot, then preheat by selecting Sauté and adjusting to Normal for
  medium heat. Cook the bacon until crisp, stirring frequently,
  then transfer to a plate with kitchen paper to blot up excess fat.
  Cancel the Sauté function. Add 200g (7oz) quick cook pasta to
  the pot and pour in 475ml (16fl oz) boiling water (there's no
  need to wash out the pot first and don't season with salt as the
  bacon has plenty). Close the lid and follow the rest of step 1,
  then steps 2 and 3 in the main recipe. When the sauce thickens,
  stir in the cooked bacon and 4 skinned, seeded and chopped
  tomatoes. Heat for a further minute, stirring.
- For Blue Cheese Pasta, follow steps 1–4 and stir in 150g (5oz)
  crumbled blue cheese such as Stilton, instead of Cheddar and
  Gruyère, in step 5.

Mushroom and Courgette Pasta ⓥ

This simple vegetarian pasta dish uses passata (ready puréed and sieved tomatoes) as a basis for the sauce. Packed with vegetables, it's a great way to get your 'five-a-day' and ideal for non-vegetarians on 'Meatless Mondays'.

SERVES 4

30ml (2 tbsp) olive oil
1 onion, finely chopped
2 cloves garlic, crushed
225g (8oz) baby button mushrooms
1 medium courgette, cut into 1cm (½in) thick round slices
1 medium carrot, grated
350ml (12fl oz) passata
300ml (½ pint) boiling vegetable stock, preferably home-made (page 45)
2.5ml (½ tsp) dried mixed herbs
Salt and freshly ground black pepper
350g (12oz) pasta, e.g. fusilli (twists) or farfalle (bows)
Freshly grated Parmesan or mature Cheddar or crumbled feta cheese, to serve (optional)

1   Preheat your Instant Pot by pressing Sauté and adjusting to Normal for medium heat. When it is hot, add the oil, then add the onion and cook for 3 minutes, stirring frequently, until beginning to soften. Add the garlic and mushrooms and cook for a further 2 minutes. Stir in the courgette and carrot.
2   Pour in the passata and stock. Add the dried herbs and season with salt and pepper. Stir well and bring to the boil. Once the sauce starts to bubble, add the pasta, stir well, then turn off the Sauté function.

3 Put on the lid and lock into place. Turn the pressure-release switch to Sealing. Press Manual (Pressure Cook), adjust the pressure to High and the time to 4 minutes. After cooking, allow the pressure to release naturally for 6 minutes, then quick-release the remaining pressure.

4 Unlock and remove the lid. Stir the pasta and adjust the seasoning, if needed. Spoon into warmed bowls. Serve scattered with grated or crumbled cheese, if liked.

Creamy Tomato and Chorizo Penne

Passata is brilliant for making smooth sauces; this one is enriched with just a little cream after cooking is complete, to make it even silkier. A really easy recipe with minimal preparation, this can be made from scratch and on the table within 30 minutes.

SERVES 4

150g (5oz) chorizo sausage, diced
1 yellow pepper, halved, seeded and cut into 2cm (¾in) chunks
100ml (4fl oz) dry white wine
350ml (12fl oz) passata
400ml (14fl oz) boiling vegetable stock, preferably home-made (page 45)
350g (12oz) dried penne pasta
Salt and freshly ground black pepper
50g (2oz) stoned olives, black or green
60ml (4 tbsp) double cream

1 Preheat your Instant Pot by pressing Sauté and adjusting to Normal for medium heat. When the pot is hot, add the chorizo and cook for 2–3 minutes, stirring frequently, until the chorizo is lightly browned. Lift the chorizo out onto a plate using a slotted spoon, leaving any fat released behind. Add the yellow pepper to the pot and cook for about 30 seconds, stirring to coat in the oil; don't let it soften or it will be overcooked in the finished dish. Add to the plate with the chorizo.

2 Pour in the wine. Let it come to the boil and bubble for 2 minutes, to evaporate the alcohol and concentrate the flavour. Pour in the passata and stock. Add the pasta and return the chorizo and yellow pepper to the pot. Stir well and season with salt and pepper. Cancel the Sauté function.

3 Put on the lid and lock into place. Turn the pressure-release switch to Sealing. Press Manual (Pressure Cook), adjust the pressure to High and the time to 4 minutes. After cooking, allow the pressure to release naturally for 6 minutes, then quick-release any remaining pressure.

4 Unlock and remove the lid. Add the olives and cream and stir into the pasta until well mixed. Serve straight away in warmed bowls.

Veggie Bean Tacos with Avocado and Lime Yogurt

Ⓥ

Crunchy corn tacos are filled with a rich chilli bean mixture and topped with a yogurt sauce. The bean filling can be made in advance and will keep in the freezer for a couple of months. You can then defrost it in the fridge overnight and reheat using the Sauté setting on your Instant Pot.

SERVES 4

For the bean tacos
15ml (1 tbsp) olive oil
1 red onion, chopped
1 clove garlic, crushed
1 red chilli, seeded and finely chopped, or 1.5ml (¼ tsp)
   dried chilli flakes
1 red or yellow pepper, halved, seeded and chopped
15ml (1 tbsp) smoked paprika
5ml (1 tsp) soft dark brown sugar
2.5ml (½ tsp) cacao or cocoa powder
400g (14oz) can chopped tomatoes
400g (14oz) can black beans, drained and rinsed, or 250g
   (9oz) cooked black beans (page 8)
Salt and freshly ground black pepper
Juice of 1 lime
156g (5oz) packet corn taco shells (12 tacos)

For the avocado and lime yogurt
1 small ripe avocado
100ml (4fl oz) Greek yogurt (page 30)
Finely grated zest of 1 lime

1   For the bean tacos, preheat your Instant Pot by pressing Sauté and adjusting to Normal for medium heat. When it is hot, add the oil, then after a few seconds, add the onion. Cook for 3–4 minutes, stirring frequently. Add the garlic, chilli and pepper and cook for a further 30 seconds, stirring. Cancel the Sauté function.
2   Sprinkle over the paprika, sugar and cacao or cocoa and stir in, then pour in the chopped tomatoes. Add the black beans, season with salt and pepper and stir well.
3   Put on the lid and lock into place. Turn the pressure-release switch to Sealing. Press Manual (Pressure Cook), adjust the pressure to High and the time to 5 minutes. After cooking, allow the pressure to release naturally for 10 minutes, then quick-release the rest.
4   Remove the lid, press Sauté and adjust to Normal for medium heat. Stir in the lime juice, then let the mixture bubble for a few minutes until very thick and spoonable. Stir frequently so that it doesn't catch on the bottom of the pan.
5   Meanwhile, heat the taco shells in the oven following the packet instructions. To make the avocado and lime yogurt, halve the avocado and remove the stone. Peel, then cut the flesh into tiny cubes. Mix with the yogurt and lime zest.
6   When ready to serve, spoon the bean mixture into the shells and top each with a spoonful of the avocado and lime yogurt.

Tofu and Quinoa Laksa

This Malaysian dish with its mildly spiced coconut sauce is usually made with fine rice noodles. Here, high-protein quinoa has been used instead to make a healthy lunch or supper dish.

SERVES 4

10ml (2 tsp) red curry paste
475ml (16fl oz) vegetable stock, preferably home-made (page 45)
1 small sweet potato, about 150g (5oz), peeled and diced
1 clove garlic, crushed
100g (4oz) quinoa, rinsed under cold water
400ml (14fl oz) can coconut milk
4 spring onions, trimmed and cut into 2cm (¾in) lengths
50g (2oz) mangetout
4 baby sweetcorn, cut in half widthways, then the larger piece halved lengthways
225g (8oz) firm tofu, cut into 2cm (¾in) cubes
45ml (3 tbsp) chopped fresh coriander

1   Put the curry paste and 60ml (4 tbsp) of the stock in your Instant Pot, then press Sauté and adjust to Less for a low heat. Stir together and cook until the mixture smells very spicy. Add the sweet potato and cook for a minute, stirring frequently. Cancel the Sauté function.
2   Add the garlic and quinoa and stir for a minute, then stir in the rest of the stock and the coconut milk, spring onions, mangetout, sweetcorn and tofu.

3 Put on the lid and lock into place. Press Manual (Pressure Cook), adjust the pressure to Low and the time to 10 minutes.

4 After cooking, allow the pressure to release naturally for 5 minutes, then quick-release the remaining pressure. Unlock and remove the lid. Stir in the chopped coriander, then ladle the laksa into warmed bowls and serve straight away.

COOK'S NOTE

- If you are vegan or vegetarian, check that the red curry paste you buy doesn't contain fish sauce. You can make your own by blending 2.5ml (½ tsp) ground cumin, 2.5ml (½ tsp) ground turmeric, 1.5ml (¼ tsp) ground coriander, 1 seeded red chilli, ½ lemon grass stalk, 1 skinned clove garlic, ½ seeded red pepper, 3 trimmed spring onions, finely grated rind of ½ lime, 45ml (3 tbsp) lime juice, 15ml (1 tbsp) sunflower oil, 5ml (1 tsp) caster or coconut sugar, 1.5ml (¼ tsp) salt and a little freshly ground black pepper to a fairly smooth paste. Store in a jar in the fridge for up to 2 weeks.

Hummus

v

Shop-bought hummus is convenient and readily available, but this protein-packed dip is so easy to make in your Instant Pot and you can adjust the flavourings to your own taste. Ready-made hummus often contains raw garlic, but here the garlic is cooked with the chickpeas, giving the hummus a more mellow and rounded flavour.

SERVES 4

150g (5oz) dried chickpeas
2 cloves garlic, left unpeeled
Juice of ½ lemon or 30ml (2 tbsp) bottled lemon juice
1.5ml (¼ tsp) ground cumin
30ml (2 tbsp) tahini
30ml (2 tbsp) natural yogurt
45ml (3 tbsp) olive oil
Salt and freshly ground black pepper

1   Dissolve 2.5ml (½ tsp) salt in 600ml (1 pint) cold water. Add the chickpeas and leave to soak overnight (you can also cook unsoaked chickpeas; see page 8).
2   The following day, drain and rinse the chickpeas and put in your Instant Pot. Pour in enough cold water to cover the peas by 1cm (½in). Add the garlic cloves.
3   Put on the lid and lock into place. Turn the pressure-release switch to Sealing. Press Manual (Pressure Cook), adjust the pressure to High and the time to 20 minutes. After cooking, allow the pressure to release naturally, then remove the lid and leave to cool for 5 minutes.

4   Drain the chickpeas, reserving about 75ml (5 tbsp) of the liquid. Tip the chickpeas into a food processor and add the reserved liquid. Squeeze the garlic out of the cloves into the processor. Process until smooth, then add the lemon juice and process again, scraping down the sides of the food processor occasionally.
5   Add the cumin, tahini, yogurt and oil. Season with a little salt and pepper. Process again; the mixture will be quite soft, but will thicken as it cools.
6   Tip and scrape the hummus into a bowl and leave until cold. Taste and adjust the seasoning if needed, or add a little more lemon juice to suit your taste. Serve straight away or cover and chill in the fridge. Use within 3 days of making.

Pearl Barley and Butternut Squash Risotto

Pearl barley makes an excellent alternative to rice when making risotto-type dishes. Here, a sprinkling of crumbled feta cheese contrasts with the sweet flavour of the butternut squash.

SERVES 4

275g (10oz) pearl barley
1 butternut squash, about 1kg (2¼lb)
15ml (1 tbsp) olive oil
1 onion, chopped
1 clove garlic, crushed
5ml (1 tsp) smoked paprika
750ml (1¼ pints) hot vegetable stock, preferably home-made (page 45)
15ml (1 tbsp) tomato purée
Salt and freshly ground black pepper
200g (7oz) feta or feta-style cheese, to serve

1 Rinse the barley in a sieve under cold running water. Tip into a bowl, cover with cold water and leave to soak for a few minutes while you prepare the vegetables.
2 Trim the top and bottom from the butternut squash and cut in half lengthways. Remove the seeds. Peel, then cut the flesh into 2cm (¾in) cubes.
3 Preheat your Instant Pot by selecting Sauté and adjust to Normal for medium heat. Add the oil and when it is hot, add the onion. Cook, stirring frequently, for 3–4 minutes. Drain the barley and add to the pot with the garlic. Stir for a minute, then sprinkle over the paprika.

4 Stir the stock and tomato purée together and add to the pot with the butternut squash. Season with salt and pepper (don't use too much salt as there is plenty in the feta).

5 Put on the lid and lock into place. Turn the pressure-release switch to Sealing. Press Steam and adjust to More. Set the time to 12 minutes. After cooking is complete, allow the pressure to release naturally for 12 minutes, then quick-release any remaining pressure.

6 Remove the lid and serve the risotto in warmed bowls, topped with a generous sprinkling of crumbled feta cheese.

Black Rice Risotto

Making risotto on the hob requires almost constant stirring. With your Instant Pot, you only need to do a little sautéing at the beginning, then you can leave your machine to finish cooking the dish.

SERVES 4

300g (11oz) Thai black rice
15ml (1 tbsp) sunflower oil
15g (½oz) unsalted butter
3 shallots, finely chopped
1 clove garlic, crushed
5ml (1 tsp) chopped fresh thyme leaves
100ml (4fl oz) dry white wine
750ml (1¼ pints) vegetable stock, preferably home-made (page 45)
Salt and freshly ground black pepper
100g (4oz) frozen peas, defrosted
75g (3oz) Parmesan cheese, grated

1   Put the rice in a bowl and pour over plenty of cold water. Leave to soak for a few minutes, while you cook the shallots.
2   Preheat your Instant Pot by pressing Sauté and adjusting to Normal for a medium heat. When the pot is hot, add the oil and butter, then add the shallots and cook for 2–3 minutes, stirring frequently, until soft.
3   Add the garlic and thyme and stir for just a few seconds. Drain the rice and add to the pot, then pour in the wine and cook for a minute, stirring frequently, to allow the alcohol to evaporate and the flavour to concentrate. Stir in the stock and season with salt (remember that the Parmesan is quite salty; you can always add more seasoning later) and black pepper. Cancel the Sauté function.

4 Put on the lid and lock into place. Turn the pressure-release switch to Sealing. Press Multigrain and adjust the pressure to High and the time to 30 minutes.

5 When cooking is complete, allow the pressure to release naturally for 10 minutes, then quick-release any remaining pressure and remove the lid. Meanwhile, put the peas in a sieve and pour over a little boiling water to warm them. Drain well and stir into the risotto.

6 Stir in about half of the grated Parmesan. Taste and adjust the seasoning if necessary. Spoon into warmed bowls and serve sprinkled with the rest of the Parmesan.

COOK'S NOTE
- If there is still too much liquid in the risotto when you remove the lid, press Sauté and adjust to Normal for a medium heat. Cook, stirring frequently to stop it catching, until it is the desired consistency.

Chicken Biryani

In this popular Indian dish, spiced chicken is cooked with a layer of basmati rice to make a complete meal. Skinless chicken thighs are a good choice as they are both inexpensive and well flavoured but use chicken breast if you prefer.

SERVES 4

200g (7oz) basmati rice
30ml (2 tbsp) ghee or 15g (½oz) unsalted butter and 15ml (1 tbsp) groundnut or sunflower oil
1 onion, halved and thinly sliced
2.5cm (1in) piece fresh ginger, finely grated
3 cloves garlic, crushed
1 red chilli, halved, seeded and finely chopped
450g (1lb) boneless, skinless chicken thighs or chicken breasts, cut into 2.5cm (1in) pieces
250ml (8fl oz) chicken or vegetable stock, preferably home-made (pages 44–45)
15ml (1 tbsp) garam masala
60ml (4 tbsp) chopped fresh coriander
30ml (2 tbsp) chopped fresh mint
Salt

1   Rinse the basmati rice in a sieve under cold running water, then tip into a bowl, add plenty of cold water and leave to soak for a few minutes.
2   Preheat your Instant Pot by selecting Sauté and adjust to Less for a low heat. Add the ghee or butter and oil and when melted, add the onion and stir to coat in the fat. Cover with a lid and cook for 5–6 minutes, stirring frequently, until soft. Add the ginger, garlic and chilli and cook for a further 2 minutes, stirring frequently, until the onion is beginning to colour at the edges.

3   Add the chicken pieces and cook for 1–2 minutes or until the outside of the chicken is opaque. Cancel the Sauté function. Stir in 30ml (2 tbsp) of the stock, then sprinkle the garam masala over the chicken, add the fresh herbs and stir well. Spread the chicken mixture out in an even layer in your Instant Pot.

4   Drain the rice, then spread out over the chicken mixture and sprinkle with a little salt. Do not stir. Pour over the remaining stock and gently push the rice down so that it is mostly covered with liquid.

5   Put on the lid and lock into place. Turn the pressure-release switch to Sealing. Press Manual (Pressure Cook), adjust the pressure to High and the time to 5 minutes.

6   When cooking is complete, allow the pressure to release naturally. Unlock the lid and serve on warmed plates, accompanied with a green vegetable such as spinach or beans and naan breads.

COOK'S NOTE
- This dish is traditionally made with whole spices, but garam masala (a blend of coriander, cumin and cardamom seeds, cloves, bay leaves, cinnamon and cayenne pepper) is a time-saving alternative.

Creole-style Prawn Gumbo

This mildly spiced rice dish comes from Louisiana and contains vegetables that the locals refer to as the 'Holy Trinity', namely onions, peppers and celery. Okra, also known as 'bhindi' in India, or 'ladies' fingers' due to its tapering shape, contains edible seeds with a thick, sticky liquid which thickens the sauce.

SERVES 4

175g (6oz) mixed basmati and wild rice
15ml (1 tbsp) olive oil
150g (5oz) chorizo sausage, finely diced
2 onions, finely chopped
2 sticks celery, chopped
2 cloves garlic, crushed
1 green pepper, halved, seeded and chopped
400g (14oz) can chopped tomatoes
750ml (1¼ pints) vegetable or chicken stock, preferably
   home-made (pages 44–45)
5ml (1 tsp) dried thyme
1 bay leaf
200g (7oz) fresh okra, thinly sliced
Salt and freshly ground black pepper
225g (8oz) large raw prawns, defrosted if frozen

1 Rinse the rice in a sieve under cold running water, then tip into a bowl, add plenty of cold water and leave to soak for a few minutes.
2 Preheat your Instant Pot by pressing Sauté and adjust to Normal for medium heat. When the pot is hot, add the oil, then add the chorizo. Cook for 3–4 minutes, stirring frequently, until it is crisp on the edges. Remove from the pot using a slotted spoon, leaving the oil behind. Drain on kitchen paper and set aside.

3 Add the onions to the pot and cook for 3–4 minutes, stirring frequently. Add the celery and garlic and cook for a further minute or until the onions are almost soft. Cancel the Sauté function.

4 Add the green pepper, tomatoes, stock, thyme, bay leaf, okra, drained rice, salt and pepper and stir well. Put on the lid and lock into place. Press Manual (Pressure Cook), adjust the pressure to High and the time to 15 minutes.

5 After cooking, allow the pressure to release naturally for 5 minutes, then quick-release the remaining pressure. Remove the lid. Press Sauté and adjust to Less for a low heat. Stir in the prawns and simmer for a minute or two, stirring frequently to stop the rice sticking, until the prawns are completely pink and cooked through. Serve straight away in warm bowls.

COOK'S NOTES
- If you can't get okra, substitute courgettes and reduce the amount of stock to 600ml (1 pint), as the sauce will thicken less.
- If you prefer, use cooked prawns (small or large) in step 5. Provided they are defrosted, simply stir them in and let the rice stand for a minute to heat them through (there's no need to reheat on the Sauté setting).

Caribbean Coconut Rice and Peas

This traditional Jamaican rice dish is made with black-eyed beans, which are known as 'peas' in the Caribbean.

SERVES 4

15ml (1 tbsp) coconut or sunflower oil
1 large onion, finely chopped
2 cloves garlic, crushed
½ red pepper, seeded and chopped
½ yellow pepper, seeded and chopped
225g (8oz) easy-cook long-grain rice, rinsed and drained
350ml (12fl oz) boiling vegetable stock, preferably home-
   made (page 45)
400ml (14fl oz) can reduced-fat coconut milk
400g can black-eyed beans, drained and rinsed,
   or 250g (9oz) cooked (page 8)
2.5ml (½ tsp) dried thyme
Salt and freshly ground black pepper

1 Preheat your Instant Pot by selecting Sauté and adjusting to Normal for medium heat. When the pot is hot, add the oil and onion and cook for 4–5 minutes until almost soft. Stir in the garlic and cook for a few more seconds. Stir in the red and yellow pepper and the rice. Cancel the Sauté function.
2 Add the stock, coconut milk, beans, thyme, salt and pepper. Stir, then put on the lid and lock into place. Turn the pressure-release switch to Sealing, press Manual (Pressure Cook) and adjust the pressure to High and the time to 3 minutes.
3 After cooking, allow the pressure to release naturally for 5 minutes, then quick-release the remaining pressure. Unlock and remove the lid. Serve straight away.

7

Vegetables

Not only are vegetables versatile, they add flavour, colour and texture to your main meal. Packed with vitamins, minerals and fibre, they are essential for a healthy diet and help you achieve the minimum recommended 'five-a-day'.

You can cook all manner of vegetables in your Instant Pot, from tender Mustard and Orange Carrots to the more robust Green Cabbage with Ginger and Spring Onions. You can also make the creamiest mashed potatoes or sweet potatoes and braises, such as Red Cabbage and Beetroot, which would usually take a couple of hours to cook conventionally, in just a few minutes. It's worth investing in an expensive steamer basket to aid lifting vegetables in and out of your inner pot. Alternatively, you might consider a multi-compartment trivet, which will keep your vegetables separate as they cook.

Remember that most vegetables cook really quickly in your Instant Pot and generally you should quick-release the pressure to prevent overcooking.

Creamy Mashed Potatoes   ⓥ

Instead of cooking potatoes in water, then draining and mashing them with hot milk and butter, cooking in your non-stick inner pot will save you time and effort and produce really creamy potatoes. Don't worry about the amount of milk; the potatoes absorb most of it as they cook.

SERVES 4

15g (½oz) unsalted butter
900g (2lb) potatoes, peeled and cut into 5cm (2in) chunks
2.5ml (½ tsp) salt
Freshly ground black pepper
250ml (8fl oz) milk

1   Cut the butter into small pieces and put in the base of your non-stick inner pot. Add the potatoes and sprinkle with salt and pepper, then pour over the milk.
2   Put on the lid and lock into place. Select Manual (Pressure Cook), adjust the pressure to High and the time to 8 minutes. After cooking, quick-release the pressure. Unlock and remove the lid.
3   Mash the potatoes into the milk mixture using a potato masher, then beat with a wooden spoon until smooth and creamy. Serve hot.

COOK'S NOTE

- These need to be cooked in a non-stick inner pot as the milk may scorch in the stainless-steel version. Use a non-scratch plastic masher to avoid damaging the non-stick coating, or tip the hot mixture into a heatproof bowl before mashing.

VARIATION

- For Garlic and Chilli Mash, add 2 peeled garlic cloves and a pinch of dried red chillies to the potatoes. Instead of butter, add 15ml (1 tbsp) olive oil.

Creamed Sweet Potatoes

These make a great change from ordinary mash and go particularly well with meats such as chicken, turkey and ham. Sweet potatoes sometimes have stringy fibres, so use a potato ricer, if you have one, to remove these and to give the finished dish a really smooth texture.

SERVES 4

About 675g (1½lb) sweet potatoes
250ml (8fl oz) water
60ml (4 tbsp) milk or single cream
15g (½oz) unsalted butter
Salt and freshly ground black pepper
1.5ml (¼ tsp) freshly grated nutmeg

1   Cut the potatoes into quarters and put in a steamer basket. Pour the water into the inner pot and lower in the basket. Put on the lid and lock into place. Select Manual (Pressure Cook), adjust the pressure to High and the time to 7 minutes. After cooking, allow the pressure to release naturally for 10 minutes, then quick-release any remaining pressure.

2   Unlock and remove the lid. Carefully lift out the steamer basket. Tip away the water in the pot and wipe dry with kitchen paper. Put the milk or cream and the butter in your Instant Pot. Select Sauté and adjust to Less for low heat. As soon as the milk is steaming and the butter has melted, press Keep Warm/Cancel.

3 Remove the skins from the sweet potatoes and using a ricer, press them into the pot. Season with salt, pepper and nutmeg, then beat with a wooden spoon for a minute or two until smooth and creamy.

COOK'S NOTE
- If you don't have a ricer, mash the potatoes and milk mixture together in the pot using a potato masher.

Potato and Onion Gratin

Cooking sliced potatoes on the Slow Cook function in your Instant Pot will ensure they are perfectly tender, yet still hold most of their shape. Most of the stock will be absorbed as they cook, so make sure you use a well-flavoured one.

SERVES 4

40g (1½oz) unsalted butter, softened
1 large onion, halved and thinly sliced
2 cloves garlic, finely chopped
900g (2lb) waxy potatoes, very thinly sliced
2.5ml (½ tsp) dried mixed herbs
Salt and freshly ground black pepper
450ml (¾ pint) vegetable stock, preferably home-made (page 45)

1   Preheat your Instant Pot by selecting Sauté and adjusting to Normal for a low heat. Add 25g (1oz) of the butter and when melted, add the onion and cook for 3–4 minutes, stirring frequently, until beginning to soften. Stir in the garlic. Cancel Sauté and remove most of the onion from the pot, leaving just a thin layer. Spoon over a little of the stock to stop the onions cooking too much.

2   Arrange an overlapping layer of potato slices on top of the onion, then sprinkle with dried herbs and a little salt and pepper. Continue layering up the ingredients, finishing with a layer of sliced potatoes. Pour over just enough of the stock to cover the potatoes. Dot the top with the remaining butter.

3 Put on the lid and lock into place. Turn the pressure-release switch to Venting. Press the Slow Cook button and adjust to Normal for medium heat. The time should automatically set to 4 hours. When cooking is complete, remove the lid and serve.

COOK'S NOTE
- This is a slow-cooked version of an oven-baked layered potato gratin. Use a cook's blowtorch if you want to to give it a lightly browned crust of the traditional dish.

Easy Jacket Potatoes

Cooking baking potatoes in your Instant Pot is much quicker than in the oven and the results are much more even than microwaving. The method and times are exactly the same if you decide to cook fewer potatoes.

SERVES 4

250ml (8fl oz) water
4 baking potatoes, about 225g (8oz) each
Salt (optional)
30ml (2 tbsp) olive oil (optional)

1   Place the trivet (steaming rack) in your Instant Pot and pour in the water. Prick each potato a few times with a fork and sprinkle with salt, if liked. Place on the rack.
2   Put on the lid and lock into place. Turn the pressure-release switch to Sealing. Select Manual (Pressure Cook) and adjust the pressure to High and the time to 10 minutes. After cooking, allow the pressure to release naturally; this can take up to 20 minutes.
3   Carefully remove the potatoes using oven gloves and serve. If you want browned crispy skins, remove the trivet (steaming rack) and tip out the water. Select Sauté and adjust to Normal for medium heat. Add the oil to the pot and when heated, add the potatoes. Cook for 3–4 minutes, turning frequently, until browned and crisp.

COOK'S NOTE
- Make sure that the potatoes are roughly the same size for even cooking and don't cook more than 2kg (4½lb) at a time.

Red Cabbage and Beetroot Braise

This is a superb accompaniment to roasted meats such as ham and turkey, and especially roast duck or goose. Red cabbage usually takes at least 2 hours to cook in the oven, but can be braised in your Instant Pot in just 20 minutes.

SERVES 4

40g (1½oz) soft light brown sugar
2.5ml (½ tsp) ground mixed spice
2.5ml (½ tsp) salt
Freshly ground black pepper
450g (1lb) red cabbage, quartered, cored and finely sliced
2 red onions, halved and thinly sliced
1 eating apple, peeled, quartered and thickly sliced
2 raw beetroot, peeled and cut into thin wedges
150ml (¼ pint) red wine
45ml (3 tbsp) red wine vinegar

1 Mix the sugar, spice, salt and pepper together. In your inner pot, layer up the cabbage, onions, apple and beetroot, sprinkling with the sugar and spice mixture between the layers. Mix together the wine and vinegar and pour over the vegetable mixture.
2 Put on the lid and lock into place. Select Manual (Pressure Cook) and adjust the pressure to High and the time to 20 minutes. After cooking, allow the pressure to release naturally for 5 minutes, then quick-release any remaining pressure.
3 Unlock and remove the lid. Stir well, taste and adjust the seasoning if necessary. Spoon into a warmed serving dish and serve hot.

Apple-glazed Brussels Sprouts

Here, Brussels sprouts are cooked with apples and apple juice to give them a delicious fruity flavour. Use even-sized fresh Brussels sprouts for the best results.

SERVES 4

15ml (1 tbsp) sunflower oil
1 small red onion, finely chopped
1 small eating apple, quartered, peeled, cored and chopped
450g (1lb) Brussels sprouts, trimmed
Salt and freshly ground black pepper
75ml (3fl oz) clear apple juice
75ml (3fl oz) vegetable stock, preferably home-made
   (page 45)
15ml (1 tbsp) cider vinegar
10ml (2 tsp) soft light brown sugar

1 Preheat your Instant Pot by selecting Sauté and adjust to Normal for medium heat. Add the sunflower oil to the inner pot and heat for a minute, then add the onion and cook, stirring frequently, for 3 minutes. Add the chopped apple and cook for a further minute, then cancel the Sauté function.
2 Add the Brussels sprouts to the pot in a steamer basket and season with salt and pepper. Pour the apple juice and stock over the sprouts.

3 Put on the lid and lock into place. Select Manual (Pressure Cook), adjust the pressure to High and the time to 1 minute. After cooking, quick-release the pressure and remove the lid. Lift out the steamer basket of sprouts; place on a plate and cover with a lid to keep them warm.

4 Select Sauté and adjust to More for high heat. Let the liquid bubble for 3–4 minutes until it thickens to a glaze. Stir in the vinegar and sugar. Return the sprouts to the pot and gently stir to coat in the glaze and reheat before serving.

Steamed Broccoli and Cauliflower ✿ with Crispy Crumbs

Steaming vegetables such as broccoli and cauliflower are simple in your Instant Pot. As well as retaining all the vitamins, it prevents your house being filled with 'cooking smells'. Use a steamer basket, so they will be kept above the water and can easily be lifted out at the end of cooking. The crispy crumb topping is optional and can be left out if you prefer.

SERVES 4

For the crispy crumb topping
30ml (2 tbsp) olive oil
100g (4oz) fresh breadcrumbs
15ml (1 tbsp) chopped fresh thyme
15ml (1 tbsp) chopped fresh parsley

For the steamed broccoli and cauliflower
175g (6oz) broccoli florets
175g (6oz) cauliflower florets
Salt and freshly ground black pepper
250ml (8fl oz) water
1 bay leaf (optional)
1 pared strip lemon or orange peel (optional)

1   To make the crispy crumb topping, preheat the inner pot by selecting the Sauté function and adjusting to Normal for a medium heat. When the inner pot is hot, add the olive oil and heat for 2 minutes. Add the breadcrumbs and cook, stirring frequently, for 4–5 minutes or until the crumbs are well browned and crisp. Cancel the Sauté function and tip the breadcrumbs onto a plate. When cool, stir in the thyme and parsley.

2   Place the broccoli and cauliflower florets stem down in a steamer basket. Season with salt and pepper. Pour the water into your Instant Pot and add the bay leaf and citrus peel, if using. Lower the basket into your Instant Pot and lock the lid into place. Select Manual (Pressure Cook), adjust the pressure to Low and the time to 3 minutes.

3   After cooking, quick-release the pressure. Unlock and remove the lid. Transfer the vegetables to a warmed served dish, sprinkle over the crumbs and serve straight away.

COOK'S NOTES
- The bay leaf and citrus peel will add very little flavour to the vegetables but smell wonderful when you open your Instant Pot and will also help stop the silicone seal from absorbing the cooking smell of cauliflower.

VARIATION
If liked, instead of the crumb topping, you can toss the cooked vegetables in a little butter and scatter with toasted almonds, or top with a cheese sauce.

Ratatouille

This classic French dish uses a mixture of colourful summer vegetables and has a wonderful fresh flavour. Once made, it can be kept in the fridge for a day or two, then gently reheated.

SERVES 4

4 ripe tomatoes
60ml (4 tbsp) olive oil
1 red onion, halved and thinly sliced
2 cloves garlic, crushed
2 aubergines, cut into 2cm (¾in) chunks
4 small courgettes, cut into 2cm (¾in) slices
2 red or yellow peppers, seeded and cut into 2cm (¾in) chunks
15ml (1 tbsp) red wine vinegar
5ml (1 tsp) caster sugar
60ml (4 tbsp) vegetable stock, preferably home-made (page 45), or water
Salt and freshly ground black pepper
60ml (4 tbsp) torn fresh basil leaves

1   Put the tomatoes in your Instant Pot and pour over just enough boiling water to cover. Leave for 1 minute, then lift out using a slotted spoon, rinse under cold water and peel off the skins (they should slip off easily). Quarter the tomatoes, scrape away and discard the seeds, then chop the flesh. Set aside. Tip out the water and wipe the inner pot dry.

2   Preheat the inner pot by selecting Sauté and adjust to Normal for medium heat. After 1 minute, add 15ml (1 tbsp) of the oil, then add the sliced onion and cook for 2–3 minutes, stirring frequently, then add the garlic and cook for a further minute. Remove from the inner pot and set aside.

3 Add the remaining 45ml (3 tbsp) oil. Heat for 1 minute, then add the aubergine chunks. Cook, stirring all the time, for 2–3 minutes until brown and beginning to soften. Add the courgettes and peppers and cook for a further minute, stirring. Return the onion to the pot, add the tomatoes, vinegar, sugar, and stock or water. Season with salt and pepper and stir well. Cancel the Sauté function.

4 Put on the lid and lock into place. Select Manual (Pressure Cook) and adjust the pressure to High and the time to 3 minutes. After cooking, quick-release the pressure. Unlock and remove the lid. Stir in the basil before serving.

Mustard and Orange Carrots

This is a simple way to give carrots extra flavour. Cooking them at low rather than high pressure will ensure they are just tender, but not overcooked. You can leave out the butter if you prefer to serve your vegetables fat-free.

SERVES 4

450g (1lb) carrots, peeled
60ml (4 tbsp) vegetable stock, preferably home-made (page 45)
Pared strip of orange zest
15g (½oz) unsalted butter
15ml (1 tbsp) orange juice (optional)
Salt and freshly ground black pepper
10ml (2 tsp) wholegrain mustard

1   Cut the carrots into thick slices or into sticks about 5cm (2in) long and place in your Instant Pot. Add the stock and orange zest, then cut the butter into tiny pieces and place on top of the carrots.
2   Put on the lid and lock into place. Press Manual (Pressure Cook), adjust the pressure to Low and the time to 4 minutes. After cooking, quick-release the pressure. Unlock and remove the lid.

3 Select Sauté and adjust to Normal for medium heat. Remove the orange zest and add the orange juice, if using. Season the carrots with salt and pepper. Bring to a boil and bubble until almost all the stock has evaporated to a thick glaze. Add the mustard and stir to coat. Serve straight away.

VARIATION
- For Lemon and Ginger Carrots, use a pared strip of lemon rind instead of the orange rind and leave out the orange juice. Finely grate a 2cm (¾ inch) piece of fresh ginger. Squeeze out the juices and add to the inner pot with the stock.

Green Beans and Shallots

This is a great vegetable dish for a special meal or dinner party, but for midweek meals you can leave out the shallots and just cook the beans on their own.

SERVES 4

175g (6oz) shallots or baby onions
15ml (1 tbsp) sunflower oil
400g (14oz) fine green beans, trimmed and cut into 5cm (2in) lengths
75ml (3fl oz) vegetable stock, preferably home-made (page 45)
Salt and freshly ground black pepper

1 Put the shallots or onions in a heatproof bowl and pour over enough boiling water to cover. Leave for 5 minutes, then drain. When cool enough to handle, remove the skins (they should slide off easily) and cut the shallots into quarters from the tip to the root end.

2 Preheat your Instant Pot by pressing Sauté and adjust to Normal for medium heat. Add the oil, then after a minute, add the shallots. Cook, stirring frequently, for 3–4 minutes or until the shallots are starting to brown a little and soften. Cancel the Sauté function.

3 Add the green beans, vegetable stock, salt and pepper. Put on the lid and lock into place. Press Manual (Pressure Cook) and adjust the pressure to High and the time to 3 minutes. After cooking, quick-release the pressure. Unlock and remove the lid. Spoon the vegetables and braising liquid into a warmed serving dish.

VARIATION
- Sliced runner beans can also be cooked in the same way; don't cut them too finely as chunkier slices work better with the browned shallots.

Braised Baby Vegetables

Ⓥ

Reducing the vegetable cooking juices and using them as a glaze not only concentrates the flavours but also retains the water-soluble vitamins.

SERVES 4

4 baby leeks, about 200g (7oz) in total
250g (9oz) baby carrots
250g (9oz) baby parsnips
15g (½oz) unsalted butter
150ml (¼ pint) vegetable stock, preferably home-made
   (page 45)
1 bay leaf
2.5ml (½ tsp) soft light brown sugar
Salt and freshly ground black pepper

1 Trim the leeks, split them lengthways, without cutting them
   completely in half, and wash well under cold running water.
   Leave the carrots whole and cut the parsnips in half
   lengthways.
2 Preheat your Instant Pot by selecting Sauté and adjusting to
   Normal for a medium heat. Add the butter and when melted,
   add the vegetables and toss to coat. Cancel the Sauté
   function. Pour in the stock and add the bay leaf.

3 Put on the lid and lock into place. Turn the pressure-release switch to Sealing. Select Manual (Pressure Cook), adjust the pressure to High and the time to 2 minutes. When cooking is complete, press Keep Warm/Cancel and quick-release the pressure. Unlock and remove the lid.

4 Press Sauté and adjust to More for a high temperature. Remove the bay leaf and sprinkle the sugar over the vegetables. Season with salt and pepper. Let the liquid boil for 2–3 minutes, or until reduced to a syrupy glaze. Remove the inner pot and tip the glazed vegetables into a warmed serving dish. Serve straight away, scattered with some chopped fresh herbs such as parsley or coriander, if desired.

Spiced Cauliflower and Potatoes

This mildly spiced dish is also known as 'aloo gobi' and is a popular choice in Indian restaurants. It goes well with all sorts of meats and vegetarian mains.

SERVES 4

15ml (1 tbsp) sunflower oil
5ml (1 tsp) cumin seeds
4 medium potatoes, about 675g (1½lb) in total, peeled and cut into 1cm (½in) slices
5ml (1 tsp) garam masala
2.5ml (½ tsp) ground turmeric
2.5ml (½ tsp) ground cumin
2.5ml (½ tsp) ground coriander
75ml (5 tbsp) tomato juice
75ml (5 tbsp) vegetable stock, preferably home-made (page 45), or water
1 medium cauliflower, divided into large florets
Salt and freshly ground black pepper
15ml (1 tbsp) chopped fresh coriander (optional), to serve

1 Preheat your Instant Pot by selecting Sauté and adjust to More for a high heat. After a couple of minutes, add the oil, allow to heat for a few seconds, then add the cumin seeds. When the seeds start to pop, add the potatoes and cook, stirring frequently, for 2–3 minutes or until they start to brown.

2 Sprinkle over the garam masala, turmeric, cumin and ground coriander. Stir well, then pour in the tomato juice and stock or water. Cancel the Sauté function. Add the cauliflower and season with salt and pepper. Gently stir everything together.

3 Put on the lid and lock into place and turn the pressure-release switch to Sealing. Select Manual (Pressure Cook), adjust the pressure to Low and the time to 2 minutes. When cooking is complete, press Cancel and quick-release the pressure. Unlock and remove the lid.

4 Spoon the potatoes and cauliflower into a warm serving dish (at this stage you can break up the florets into slightly smaller pieces, if you prefer). Serve scattered with chopped fresh coriander, if using.

Green Cabbage with Ginger and Spring Onions

Cabbage should never be boiled in masses of water or served soggy. Your Instant Pot ensures that it retains a slight 'bite' and that all the vitamins and minerals are preserved. An added hint of ginger and garlic enhances the flavour.

SERVES 4

15ml (1 tbsp) sunflower oil
6 spring onions, thinly sliced
1 clove garlic, crushed
2cm (¾in) piece fresh ginger, peeled and grated
Small green cabbage, quartered, central core removed, and finely shredded
Salt and freshly ground black pepper
75ml (5 tbsp) vegetable stock, preferably home-made (page 45), or water

1   Preheat your Instant Pot by selecting Sauté and adjust to Normal for a medium heat. After a couple of minutes, add the oil, allow to heat for a few seconds, then add the spring onions. Cook for 2 minutes, stirring frequently, then add the garlic and ginger and stir for a few more seconds.

2   Cancel the Sauté function. Add the shredded cabbage to the pot, season with salt and pepper and mix well. Pour over the stock or water.

3   Put on the lid and lock into place. Turn the pressure-release switch to Sealing. Select Manual (Pressure Cook), adjust the pressure to High and the time to 1 minute. When cooking is complete, press Keep Warm/Cancel and quick-release the pressure. Unlock and remove the lid. Serve the cabbage straight away.

8

Desserts and Bakes

By the time you reach this chapter, you'll have discovered that your Instant Pot makes tasty soups, suppers and main meals, and cooks rice and pasta to perfection. However, you can also use your machine to create delicious desserts and bakes. While some are indulgent and should perhaps only be served as occasional treats, there are also healthier versions of classic favourites, including chocolate brownies made with starchy black beans rather than flour for a protein-packed treat, and a crème 'caramel' made by caramelising apple juice rather than pure sugar. From Cherry and Almond Cheesecake and Creamy Rice Pudding to Banana and Butternut Squash Cake and Sticky Ginger Cake, this tempting chapter is perfect for anyone with a sweet tooth.

Cherry and Almond Cheesecake Ⓥ

The steamy environment of your Instant Pot is perfect for making smooth and creamy cheesecakes. This light version is made with ricotta, which is lower in fat than cream cheese, and has a thin amaretti biscuit base that gives it a distinctive almond flavour.

SERVES 6–8

40g (1½oz) unsalted butter, plus extra for greasing
100g (4oz) amaretti biscuits, crushed
350g (12oz) ricotta cheese
65g (2½oz) caster sugar
2 medium eggs, beaten
10ml (2 tsp) pure vanilla extract
60ml (4 tbsp) ground almonds
250ml (8fl oz) water

For the topping
400g (14oz) frozen pitted cherries, defrosted
5ml (1 tsp) cornflour
10ml (2 tsp) caster sugar

1 Line the bottom of a non-stick 20cm (8in) round loose-bottomed tin with baking parchment. Lightly brush with a little melted butter (or use melted coconut oil if you prefer). Put the tin on a piece of foil and fold up the sides (this will stop the steam making the base soggy as it cooks).

2 Put the butter in your inner pot. Press Sauté and adjust to Less for a low heat. When melted, cancel the Sauté function. Stir in the crushed amaretti biscuits. Spoon the mixture into the base of the prepared tin and press with the back of a spoon into a thin even layer. Wipe out your inner pot with kitchen paper.

3   Put the ricotta cheese in a fine stainless-steel or nylon sieve and press it through the sieve into a bowl. Beat the sugar and eggs in another bowl until fairly thick and frothy. Stir the vanilla extract into the ricotta, then gradually beat the egg mixture into the ricotta cheese. Sprinkle over the ground almonds and stir into the mixture. Pour the mixture into the tin. Cover the tin tightly with foil, doming it slightly as the cheesecake will rise a little then fall as it cooks.

4   Place the trivet (steaming rack) in your Instant Pot and pour in the water. Lower the tin into your Instant Pot using a foil sling (see page 6). Put on the lid and lock into place, turn the pressure-release switch to Sealing and press Manual (Pressure Cook). Adjust the pressure to High and the time to 15 minutes.

5   After cooking, allow the pressure to release naturally for 10 minutes, then quick-release any remaining pressure. Remove the lid, carefully remove the cheesecake from the pot and remove the foil covering. The cheesecake should be barely set, and will firm as it cools. When cold, chill in the fridge, preferably overnight.

6   No more than a few hours before serving, make the topping. Tip the defrosted cherries into a sieve placed over the inner pot and allow the juices to drip through into the pot. Add the cornflour and sugar to the juices and stir with a wooden spoon to blend, then add the cherries. Press Sauté and adjust to Normal for a medium heat. Bring to the boil and bubble for 1 minute, stirring until thickened. Cancel the Sauté function and leave until just cool, stirring occasionally.

7   Spoon the cooled topping over the cheesecake and return it to the fridge to allow it to set. Before serving, carefully remove the cheesecake from the tin and transfer to a serving plate.

Apple and Honey Crème Caramel Ⓥ

This light version of crème caramel uses reduced apple juice and honey instead of a sugar caramel. Served with fresh fruit, it makes a healthy dessert and any leftovers can be eaten for a guilt-free breakfast. Here, your Instant Pot is used as a 'bain marie' by steaming the pudding using the Sauté function.

SERVES 4

300ml (½ pint) clear apple juice
45ml (3 tbsp) clear honey
500ml (16fl oz) full-fat milk
3 medium eggs
5ml (1 tsp) vanilla extract
500ml (16fl oz) boiling water

1   Pour the apple juice into your inner pot and add 7.5ml (1½ tsp) of the honey. Press Sauté and adjust to More for a high heat. Let the mixture boil rapidly for about 10 minutes or until reduced to a thick glaze, about 90ml (6 tbsp). Watch it carefully towards the end as it can burn easily; turn off the Sauté function a few minutes before it has become too thick.

2   Pour the thickened apple syrup into a 900ml (1½ pint) soufflé dish (make sure it will fit into your Instant Pot first). Swirl the mixture so that it coats the base and partway up the sides of the dish. Leave to cool.

3   Pour the milk into the inner pot (there's no need to wash it out first). Press Sauté and adjust to More for a high heat. When the milk is steaming hot, cancel the Sauté function. Meanwhile, using an electric whisk, beat the remaining honey and the eggs together in a bowl until creamy. Add the vanilla extract and whisk for a few more seconds.

4   Pour the hot milk over the egg and honey mixture, whisking as you pour. Wash the inner pot and return it to your Instant Pot. Add the trivet (steaming rack) and pour in the boiling water.

5   Pour the egg and honey mixture into the soufflé dish and cover the top with foil. Lower into your Instant Pot using a foil sling (see page 6).

6   Put on the lid and lock into place, then turn the pressure-release switch to Venting. Select Sauté and adjust to More for a high heat. Set a timer for 20 minutes (as you're not using the pressure-cooking function, your Instant Pot will not work as a timer).

7   When cooking is complete, turn off your Instant Pot and leave for a further 5 minutes. Unlock and remove the lid. Check that the custard is cooked by inserting a thin knife into the middle; the custard should be wobbly, but the knife should come out clean. If not, put the lid back on, press Sauté and cook for a further 5 minutes.

8   Remove the custard and leave until completely cool, then chill in the fridge for 4 hours. Loosen the edges with a blunt knife, place a plate on top of the dish and invert to turn out.

Creamy Rice Pudding

Oven-baked rice pudding is thick and creamy due to the concentration of the milk, as water evaporates during the long slow cooking. You can achieve exactly the same consistency by using evaporated milk in your Instant Pot but in a fraction of the time. This very simple version is made without added sugar, so serve with maple syrup, brown sugar or a spoonful of jam if you have a sweet tooth.

SERVES 4

100g (4oz) pudding rice
400ml (14fl oz) can evaporated milk (light version, if you prefer)
300ml (½ pint) full-fat or semi-skimmed milk
Pinch of freshly grated nutmeg

1   Put the rice, evaporated milk and whole or semi-skimmed milk in your Instant Pot (a non-stick inner pot is best for this). Press Sauté and adjust to Less for a low heat. Leave for 10 minutes for the milk to warm and the rice to start absorbing the liquid. Cancel the Sauté function.
2   Stir the rice and milk well, making sure that the rice isn't stuck to the bottom of the pot. Put on the lid and lock into place. Turn the pressure-release switch to Sealing. Press Manual (Pressure Cook) and set to Low for 12 minutes.
3   When cooking is complete, allow the pressure to release naturally. Remove the lid, give the rice a stir and serve straight away, or if preferred allow to cool and store in the fridge for up to 2 days.

COOK'S NOTE
- If liked, spoon the pudding into a heatproof serving dish, sprinkle the top with sugar and brown under a hot grill.

VARIATIONS
- For Coconut Rice Pudding, use a 400ml (14fl oz) can coconut milk instead of the evaporated milk and follow the main recipe.
- For Plum, Rum and Raisin Rice Pudding, put 25g (1oz) raisins in a small bowl and spoon over 30ml (2 tbsp) dark rum. Quarter 4 ripe plums and remove the stones. Put in the inner pot with 60ml (4 tbsp) water and 10ml (2 tsp) soft light brown sugar. Press Sauté and adjust to Less for a low heat. Let the plums come to a gentle simmer and cook for 4–5 minutes, stirring until softened but still holding their shape. Add a little extra water if needed, depending on how juicy the plums are. Remove from the inner pot and set aside. Make the rice pudding as the main recipe (there's no need to wash out the pot). Stir the raisins and any rum that hasn't been soaked up into the rice pudding, then spoon the rice pudding into individual heatproof glasses or bowls. Serve topped with the plum compote.

Blushing Poached Pears

Here fresh pears take on a pretty pink hue from the wine to make a stunning dinner-party dessert. Make sure you bring the wine to the boil first to allow the alcohol to evaporate or you will have a very potent pudding!

SERVES 6

1 bottle sweet rosé wine
25–50g (1–2oz) caster sugar
45ml (3 tbsp) clear honey
1 vanilla pod, split lengthways
Large strip of orange zest
2 whole cloves
6 firm ripe pears
Juice of ½ lemon
Fresh bay leaves or mint leaves, to garnish

1   Pour the wine into your Instant Pot. Add the sugar, honey, vanilla pod, orange zest and cloves. Press Sauté and adjust to More for a high heat. As the mixture warms, stir occasionally until the sugar dissolves. Bring the wine to the boil and let it bubble for 2–3 minutes to allow the alcohol to evaporate, then cancel the Sauté function.

2   Meanwhile, peel the pears, leaving the stem intact. Use an apple corer to carefully remove the core from the middle of the pears. Cut a very thin slice off the base of each pear so that it will stand square and upright when served. As each pear is peeled, toss in lemon juice to prevent it from going brown.

3 Place the pears in the spiced wine mixture, packing them tightly together and upright. Put on the lid and lock into place. Turn the pressure-release switch to Sealing. Press Manual (Pressure Cook), adjust the pressure to High and the time to 3 minutes. After cooking, allow the pressure to release naturally for 5 minutes, then quick-release the remaining pressure. Unlock and remove the lid.

4 Carefully lift out the pears using a slotted spoon and place in a serving dish. Press Sauté and adjust to More for a high heat. Let the wine mixture bubble until thicker and more syrupy and reduced to about half of its original volume. Leave the syrup to cool, then strain over the pears to remove the vanilla pod, orange zest and cloves. Chill in the fridge.

5 Serve the pears lightly chilled or at room temperature (take out of the fridge about an hour before serving). Place each upright in a bowl, spooning over some rosé wine syrup and garnishing each with a bay or mint leaf.

COOK'S NOTE
- The cooking time will depend on the ripeness of your pears. They should be tender all the way through when tested with a cocktail stick. If they are not quite done, leave them in the liquid and cook for a few more minutes using the Sauté setting adjusted to Less for a low heat. Keep the lid off during this time so that the liquid starts to evaporate.

VARIATION
- For Ruby Poached Pears, use 600ml (1 pint) red grape juice and 75ml (5 tbsp) ruby port instead of the rosé wine and follow the main recipe.

Dulce de Leche

(V)

Dulce de leche is simply caramelised condensed milk. It is high in sugar, so should only be an occasional indulgent treat. It can be diluted with a little milk to make a delicious sauce for desserts such as ice cream, used as a cake filling or thinly spread on buttered toast. It's probably most famous for its use in banoffee pie.

MAKES 400G (14OZ)

397g (14oz) can sweetened condensed milk
2.5ml (½ tsp) bicarbonate of soda
30ml (2 tbsp) warm water

1 Pour the condensed milk into a stainless-steel bowl which fits into your Instant Pot, about 18cm (7in) wide and at least 9cm (3½in) deep is ideal. Mix the bicarbonate of soda and warm water together in a small bowl. Add to the condensed milk and stir well. Cover the top tightly with foil.

2 Pour 250ml (8fl oz) water into your Instant Pot, then place the bowl of condensed milk directly into the water (there's no need to use a trivet). Put on the lid and lock into place. Turn the pressure-release switch to Sealing. Press Manual (Pressure Cook), adjust the pressure to High and the time to 40 minutes.

3 After cooking, allow the pressure to release naturally, then remove the lid. Lift out the bowl; the dulce de leche will be quite lumpy, so give it a good whisk. Leave to cool. It will keep for up to 4 weeks in the fridge.

COOK'S NOTE

- To make a slightly lighter version of a Banoffee Pie, stir 45ml (3 tbsp) half-fat crème fraiche into the dulce de leche. Spoon into a 20–22cm (8–8½in) ready-made unsweetened pastry case and level smooth with the back of the spoon. Sprinkle 1.5ml (¼ tsp) coffee granules and 10ml (2 tsp) caster sugar, preferably unrefined, over 150ml (¼ pint) whipping cream. Whisk until soft peaks form. Mix together 200g (7oz) Greek yogurt (page 31) and 45ml (3 tbsp) half-fat crème fraiche and fold into the whipped cream. Peel and slice a large ripe banana and toss the slices in lemon juice. Arrange on top of the dulce de leche. Spoon the whipped cream mixture on top and dust with 2.5ml (½ tsp) cacao or unsweetened cocoa powder before serving.

Banana and Butternut Squash Cake

Cooking a cake on the Slow Cook setting allows all the flavours to develop while keeping it moist at the same time. Unlike oven-baked cakes, the mixture rises evenly, giving you a beautifully flat top should you wish to ice the cake instead of dusting with icing sugar.

SERVES 8–12

125g (4½oz)t soft light brown sugar
100ml (4fl oz) melted coconut oil or sunflower oil, plus extra for greasing
2 medium eggs, beaten
2 medium, very ripe bananas, mashed
100g (4oz) coarsely grated butternut squash
225g (8oz) self-raising flour
5ml (1 tsp) baking powder
10ml (2 tsp) ground cinnamon
Pinch of salt
15ml (1 tbsp) icing sugar, to dust

1 Line the base and grease a 20cm (8in) fixed-based round cake tin, about 8cm (3in) deep. Make a foil sling (see page 6).
2 Mix the sugar and oil together in a bowl, then gradually beat in the eggs; the mixture should look like thick toffee. Stir in the mashed bananas and grated butternut squash.

3   Sift the flour, baking powder, cinnamon and salt into the bowl and gently mix everything together. Spoon and scrape the mixture into the prepared tin. Cover the top of the tin tightly with foil.

4   Put the trivet (steaming rack) into the bottom of the inner pot (leave it folded or you won't be able to fit the cake tin in the pot) and pour in enough boiling water to come just over the 1½-litre mark. Lower the cake into the pot using the foil sling: the water should come about halfway up the tin.

5   Put on the lid and turn the pressure-release switch to Venting. Press the Slow Cook button and then adjust the temperature to More. The time will automatically set to 4 hours and will count down during cooking.

6   When cooking is complete, remove the lid and lift out the cake using the foil sling. Remove the foil from the top of the tin to allow steam to escape and place on a wire rack. Leave to cool in the tin for 5 minutes before turning out. Leave the cake to cool completely, then thickly dust the top with icing sugar or ice the cake, if preferred, before serving.

Black Bean Brownies

Similar brownies to this flour-free version are sold in health food stores and vegetarian cafes throughout the country. No one will know they contain pulses unless you tell them; the beans simply add texture to the brownies and work as a flour substitute. Cooking in your Instant Pot makes them beautifully moist and they make a great high-protein treat, perfect for a healthy snack.

SERVES 8

250g (9oz) cooked black beans (page 8)
2 medium eggs
40g (1½oz) cacao or unsweetened cocoa powder, sifted
75ml (3fl oz) maple syrup
15ml (1 tbsp) vanilla extract
Pinch of salt
100g (4oz) coconut oil, melted if solid, plus extra for greasing
75g (3oz) toasted nuts, such as chopped walnuts or flaked almonds (optional)
250ml (8fl oz) cold water
2.5ml (½ tsp) icing sugar, to dust

1   Line the base and grease an 18cm (7in) round fixed-based cake tin, about 8cm (3in) deep. Make a foil sling (see page 6).

2   Put the beans, eggs, cacao or cocoa, maple syrup, vanilla and salt in a food processor and blend until fairly smooth. Slowly add the melted coconut oil while the machine is running. Continue to process for 3–4 minutes until the mixture lightens slightly and is a little airier in texture. Add about half of the nuts, if using, and very briefly blend again just to combine them.

3   Spoon and scrape the mixture into the prepared tin and level the top. Scatter over the remaining nuts. Cover the top of the tin tightly with foil.

4   Put the trivet (steaming rack) into the bottom of the inner pot (leave it folded or you won't be able to fit the cake tin in the pot) and pour in the cold water. Lower the cake into the pot using the foil sling.

5   Put on the lid and lock into place. Turn the pressure-release switch to Sealing. Press Manual (Pressure Cook) and adjust the pressure to High and the time to 18 minutes.

6   When cooking is complete, allow the pressure to release naturally for 15 minutes, then quick-release any remaining pressure. Remove the lid and lift out the cake using the foil sling. Remove the foil from the top of the tin to allow steam to escape and place on a wire rack. Leave to cool in the tin for 5 minutes before turning out. Dust the top with icing sugar and cool completely before slicing.

Sticky Ginger Cake

The Slow Cook function on your Instant Pot is perfect for making this tea-time treat. Usually ginger cake is left for a day or two to 'mature' before eating, but slow cooking will do this for you. This should be served in small portions as it is fairly high in sugar; however, it does contain black treacle, which is a great source of iron.

SERVES 8–10

450ml (¾ pint) boiling water, plus a little extra
150g (5oz) light muscovado sugar
85g (3½oz) butter or coconut oil, plus extra for greasing
100g (4oz) golden syrup
75g (3oz) black treacle
175g (6oz) self-raising flour
50g (2oz) wholemeal flour
10ml (2 tsp) ground ginger
5ml (1 tsp) ground cinnamon
Pinch of salt
1 medium egg, lightly beaten
100ml (4fl oz) milk, at room temperature
2.5ml (½ tsp) bicarbonate of soda

1 Line the base and grease a 20cm (8in) round fixed-based cake tin, about 8cm (3in) deep. Make a foil sling (see page 6).

2 Pour the boiling water into the inner pot. Put the sugar, butter or coconut oil, syrup and treacle in a heatproof bowl that will fit inside the inner pot (and be easy to lift in and out). Place in the inner pot (the water should come no more than halfway up the bowl). Leave for about 10 minutes until melted, stirring occasionally.

3   Remove the bowl from the inner pot. Sift the flours, ginger, cinnamon and salt over the melted mixture, tipping in the bran from the wholemeal flour left in the sieve. Add the beaten egg and stir together (there's no need to mix it completely at this stage). Stir the bicarbonate of soda into the milk, add to the ginger-cake mixture and stir together until thoroughly combined. Pour into the prepared tin and cover the top with foil.

4   Place the trivet (steaming rack) in the inner pot and lower in the cake tin, using the foil sling. Very carefully pour in a little more boiling water around the tin, so that the water comes just above halfway up the sides.

5   Put on the lid and lock into place. Turn the pressure-release switch to Venting. Press the Slow Cook button and adjust to More for a high heat and the time to 3 hours.

6   When cooking is complete, remove the lid, lift out the cake using the foil sling and place the tin on a cooling rack. Remove the foil covering and leave to cool for 15 minutes, then turn out and leave to cool completely before serving.

COOK'S NOTES

- If you don't have a fixed-based 20cm (8in) round cake tin, you can use a soufflé dish or round casserole dish of the same size. Add an extra 15 minutes to the cooking time, as it will take longer for heat to penetrate through the dish.
- Although the ginger cake will be ready to eat as soon as it is cool, the texture and flavour will improve if wrapped and kept for a day or two.

Spiced Apple Cake

ⓥ

In Germany, this moist spicy *apfelkuchen* can be enjoyed in tea and coffee houses everywhere. It's often topped with overlapping slices of apple, but here it's finished more simply with a dusting of icing sugar.

SERVES 12

100g (4oz) plain flour
100g (4oz) wholemeal flour
10ml (2 tsp) baking powder
10ml (2 tsp) ground cinnamon
2.5ml (½ tsp) ground ginger
75g (3oz) butter, softened, plus extra for greasing
150g (5oz) soft light brown sugar
Finely grated zest of 1 small orange
2 medium eggs, beaten
2 medium eating apples, peeled, quartered, cored and chopped
300ml (½ pint) boiling water
5ml (1 tsp) icing sugar, to dust

1   Line the base and grease a 20cm (8in) round fixed-based cake tin, about 8cm (3in) deep. Make a foil sling (see page 6).
2   Sift the flours, baking powder and spices together in a bowl, adding the bran left in the sieve. Put the butter, sugar and orange zest in another bowl and beat together until light and fluffy. Beat in the eggs, a little at the time, then sift over most of the flour mixture, reserving about 30ml (2 tbsp).

3 Add the chopped apples to the reserved flour mixture, and toss together to coat. Start folding the flour mixture into the beaten egg mixture, then, when almost mixed, add the coated apple chunks and mix again until fully combined.

4 Spoon the mixture into the cake tin and level the surface. Cover the tin with foil. Place the trivet (steaming rack) in the bottom of your Instant Pot and pour in the boiling water. Carefully lower the cake into the pot using the foil sling.

5 Put on the lid and lock into place. Turn the pressure-release switch to Sealing. Press Manual (Pressure Cook), adjust the pressure to High and the time to 25 minutes. After cooking, allow the pressure to release naturally for 10 minutes, then quick-release the remaining pressure. Unlock and remove the lid.

6 Lift out the cake and leave to cool in the tin for 10 minutes before turning out and cooling on a wire rack. Lightly dust the top with icing sugar before slicing and serving.

Cornbread

This golden savoury bake makes a quick-cook alternative to bread. It comes from America's Deep South and is traditionally served with dishes such as chilli con carne (page 82).

SERVES 4–6

Melted unsalted butter or coconut oil, to grease
125g (4½oz) fine cornmeal
250ml (8fl oz) cold water
75g (3oz) plain flour
10ml (2 tsp) baking powder
2.5ml (½ tsp) salt
5ml (1 tsp) caster sugar
1 medium egg
280ml (9fl oz) carton buttermilk
1 small mild green or red chilli, halved, seeded and very
   finely chopped

1 Line the bottom of a non-stick 18cm (7in) round loose-bottomed round tin with baking parchment. Lightly brush with melted unsalted butter or coconut oil. Sprinkle 10ml (2 tsp) of the cornmeal into the tin, then turn the tin to coat the base and sides evenly.
2 Put the steaming rack (trivet) in the base of your Instant Pot and pour in the cold water. Put the remaining cornmeal, flour, baking powder, salt and sugar in a mixing bowl and stir together. Make a small hollow in the middle.

3 Whisk the egg and buttermilk together in a jug. Pour the egg mixture into the hollow, add the chilli and quickly stir together to make a thick batter; do not overmix or the bread will be tough. Spoon and scrape into the prepared tin and level the surface. Cover with foil and using a foil sling (see page 6), lower the tin into your Instant Pot.

4 Put on the lid, lock into place and turn the pressure-release switch to Sealing. Press Manual (Pressure Cook), adjust the pressure to High and the time to 20 minutes.

5 After cooking, allow the pressure to release naturally for 5 minutes, then quick-release the remaining pressure. Remove the lid, lift out the cornbread, allow to cool for a few minutes in the tin, then turn out onto a wire rack. Cut into wedges and serve warm.

COOK'S NOTES

- Cornmeal is sometimes labelled 'fine polenta'. You can substitute fine semolina for cornmeal, although the colour of the bread will be paler and the flavour slightly different.
- Instead of buttermilk, you can use milk and lemon juice. Stir 5ml (1 tsp) lemon juice into 280ml (9fl oz) semi-skimmed milk. Leave at room temperature for 20 minutes before using to allow the milk to thicken a little.

Index